Classical Polyphony

P. SAMUEL RUBIO

Classical Polyphony

TRANSLATED BY

THOMAS RIVE

Associate-Professor of Music in the
University of Auckland, New Zealand

UNIVERSITY OF TORONTO PRESS

First published in Canada and the United States
by University of Toronto Press,
Toronto and Buffalo

ISBN 0-8020-1681-2
ISBN (microfiche) 0-8020-0094-0

Translated, with permission, from the Spanish edition
La Polifonía Clásica
Biblioteca 'La Ciudad de Dios'
El Escorial, 1956

Printed in Great Britain

Contents

Part I Paleography

1 VARIOUS CONVENTIONS AND SIGNS USED IN WRITING

The voices, 3. The disposition of voices in manuscripts and printed editions, 3. The clefs, 5. Canon, 6. The direct, 7. The pause, 7. Repeat marks, 8. The flat, sharp and natural, 8.

2 THE NOTATION OF POLYPHONY

The notes and rests, 10. Note-values in relation to each other, 11.

3 NOTE-VALUES IN RELATION TO THE BAR

The bars in use during the sixteenth century, 14. The existence of the ternary bar in the sixteenth century, 15.

4 THE NUMBER OF NOTES IN EACH BAR AND IN EACH OF ITS PARTS

The sign of time imperfect (*tempus imperfectus*), 18. The sign of time perfect (*tempus perfectus*), 20. Prolation, 24.

5 THE PROPORTIONS

The signs of time perfect and time imperfect accompanied by proportional numbers, 28. Proportional signs by themselves, 30. Ligatures, 32.

Appendix

OBSERVATIONS ON THE INTERPRETATION OF POLYPHONY

The meaning of the word 'interpretation', 129. General principles, 130. Expression, 131. Tessitura, 131. Tempo, 132. Colour, 134.

Plates

Author's Foreword

This book seeks to throw light on the study of classical polyphony, and to open the way to all who wish to gain direct knowledge of the secrets preserved within its staves.

When, for the first time, anyone picks up a piece of polyphonic music—manuscript or printed—in order to decipher its contents, he is immediately faced with a number of problems which may well compel him to abandon the project. There are signs he does not understand; notes of unknown shape and value; here and there appear phrases of music without any verbal text. And this is not the most serious aspect of the case, though it is bad enough. These difficulties, like declared enemies, are immediately obvious, and can be wrestled with by studying the treatises of the period.

But in the documents of polyphony there are hidden problems, difficult to discover and hence to deal with. Frequently signs are not given and have to be added, and what complicates the situation is that nowhere is there any indication that they are missing. We refer to sharps and flats, in time-honoured terminology the 'semitonía subintellecta' (i.e. implied or understood chromatic alteration), a problem which can easily give the uninitiated the impression of a false modality.

Apart from these conventions of notation found in polyphony, there are, as in all art, others deriving from its essential nature, its internal architecture—in technical terms, from its musical forms. The object of the present book, the first to be published in Spain in modern times dealing with these matters, is to explain these difficulties.

We shall not repeat the hackneyed phrase that, with this book, we hope to supply a need. But it must be confessed that there does not exist, in Spanish, a handbook which gives elementary instruction on the art of polyphony. This deficiency has been pointed out and its remedy urged by the Popes Pius X and XI, and recently by Pius XII.

Since Eslava embarked on musicological studies with the publication of his *Lira Sacra Hispana*, editions of Spanish music from the sixteenth and seventeenth centuries have followed, at more or less frequent intervals. But, in contrast to what happens in other countries, theoretical and technical studies in the same material have not made even the most tentative appearance in Spain. A quick glance at the bibliography given at the end of this book will be enough to show, in marked contrast to the current scarcity, the number of Spanish treatises written in previous centuries.

It is possible that no work on the notation of Renaissance polyphony has been written in Spain since that published in 1762 by P. Antonio Soler—his very widely-used *Llave de la modulación y antigüedades de la música* (Key to modulation and early practice in music).

*   *   *

This book is in two parts. In the first the meaning of all the signs used in the sixteenth century in the writing of vocal music is explained. The problems raised by its transcription into modern scores are stated, and solutions given which we feel conform most closely to historical truth. Briefly its purpose is to demonstrate the art of deciphering every detail of any document of classical vocal polyphony. It is, accordingly, entitled *Paleography*.

Bearing in mind the possibility that some of our statements may sound to some readers like the sharpest and most strident dissonance, we have thought it advisable to quote in confirmation—like a sweet-toned mute—whole pages from the most learned writers of the fifteenth and sixteenth centuries. (This has been done because it is almost impossible for most readers to consult extremely rare works for purposes of study and discussion.) In this way anyone may judge for himself whether the opinions we favour are completely unfounded or, on the contrary, based on sound premises.

The second part of the book is devoted to the *Musical Forms of Polyphony*, without the study of which it is impossible to gain a true idea of its perfection and beauty.

Just as an architect tests his building materials with the idea of gaining a thorough knowledge of his structure, we begin by analysing the various elements of construction in the art of polyphony, so that it will be possible to see later how, by putting these together, the polyphonic composers erected their magnificent edifices of sound.

In the second, as in the first part, we frequently rely on examples to clarify our explanations; there is no better method when it comes to dealing with musical subjects.

Towards the end of the book we devote some pages to the interpretation of polyphony. This has been done at the suggestion of our students in the well-known summer courses in the Escorial and at Vitoria, and it is to them principally that they are dedicated.

God grant that this work will contribute to the greater knowledge and wider diffusion of Classical Polyphony, one of the most perfect branches of the art of sacred music, and thus to the exalting of the prayer sung in His praise.

Translator's Foreword and Acknowledgements

In writing a foreword to the English translation of *La Polifonía Clásica* by P. Samuel Rubio, O.S.A., acknowledgement must be made of the author's eminence in the field of Renaissance musical scholarship. Students of sixteenth-century polyphony have reason to be grateful both for scholarly articles such as have appeared in "La Ciudad de Dios" and for his editing of such collections as *Antología Polifónica Sacra* (Madrid, 1954–56), *Canciones Espirituales* (Madrid, 1955–56) and Tomás Luis de Victoria, *Motetes* Vols. 1–4 (Madrid, 1964). His experience as Maestro de Capilla de El Real Monasterio de El Escorial underlines the fact that he is an able and accomplished practising musician.

His Spanish origin and emphasis are immediately obvious. Indeed he makes it quite clear in his own foreword that the book was written primarily for home consumption. It soon becomes equally obvious that this emphasis is by no means exclusive. In any case, Spanish music must loom large in any study of the Renaissance period and, this being so, the Spanish theoretical point of view is also important. Accordingly, Bermudo, Santa María, Tapia and Tovar are quoted extensively along with Vanneo, Vicentino, Zacconi and Zarlino.

If in respect of theoretical quotation Spaniards are simply among those present, in music reference and quotation they are in a handsome majority. But even this merely serves to emphasize that these composers made their strongly national and personal contribution to the composition of liturgical polyphony within the bounds of a widely-used *lingua franca*. A Spanish accent is discernible, but the vocabulary and syntax are basically identical with those of the composers of the Roman school.

The book's concern is with the music of the period, as it was disseminated in the period, and its technical discussion deals with this music in the light of contemporary music theory, rather than from a twentieth-century point of view. It should, in translation, serve to supplement text-books dealing more specifically with the grammar of the style.

I should like to acknowledge, with gratitude, the courtesy and assistance received from Father Rubio, both by correspondence and during consultations in Rome, January 1966, and at El Real Monasterio de El Escorial in October 1971. *La Polifonía Clásica* is for him not only a supremely fascinating and expressive musical style, but still a living language of Christian devotion, and I hope I have been able to communicate not only the substance but also something of the spirit of his writing on this subject.

My sincere thanks for assistance and advice are offered to Mrs. Shirley Clarke of Aberdeen, Scotland (formerly of Auckland), Miss Olive Johnson, of the University of Auckland Library, and Miss Rosemary Nalden and Mr. David Nalden of London (both formerly of Auckland).

I must also record my appreciation of the understanding acquiescence of Mr. John Cutforth, of Basil Blackwell, in my suggestion that the various passages from sixteenth-century authors be included in the *Notes*, in their original languages, as well as in the main text, translated.

Thomas Rive,
Conservatorium of Music,
The University of Auckland,
Auckland, New Zealand

Publisher's Note

The same blocks have been used for the printing of music examples as in the original edition. A glossary of abbreviations, words and phrases in these examples is given below. These are in Spanish unless otherwise indicated.

Abbreviations— c. (compás, compases) = bar, bars
2^a. (segunda) = second
3^a. (tercera) = third
5^a. (quinta) = fifth
6^a. (sexta) = sixth
8^a. (octava) = octave

Note-values—
máxima = large
longa = long
breve = breve
semibreve = semibreve
mínima = minim
semínima = crotchet
corchea = quaver
semicorchea = semiquaver

Other words and Phrases— aumentada = augmented
mayor = major
menor = minor
non buona (It.) = poor
perfecta = perfect
per bisogna (It.) = only if unavoidable

así = thus / o así = or thus / no así = not thus
escritura = written / efecto = sounding
dos negras in dos movimientos = two crotchets in two beats
tres negras in dos movimientos = three crotchets in two beats
Regola universale di porre la parole sotto alle note (It.) = a summary of the procedure for underlaying of text.

Agenda defunctorum

E quando rapiat vt leo animã meam animã meam, dñ nõ eft qui redimat qui redimat ñ neq. qui faluum faciat faciat.

Altus.

E quãdo ra pi at vt leo animã meam ñ dñ nõ eft qui redimat qui redimat, qui redimat neq. qui faluñ faciat qui faluñ faciat.

Tenor.

E quando ra pi at vt le o a ni mã me am dñ non eft qui re di mat ne q. qui faluum faciat.

Bafis.

E quãdo rapiat vt leo animã meam animã me am dñ nõ eft qui redimat qui re dimat neq. qui faluñ faciat faciat.

Ad porta inferi. Erue domine animas eorum. Pater nofter.

II

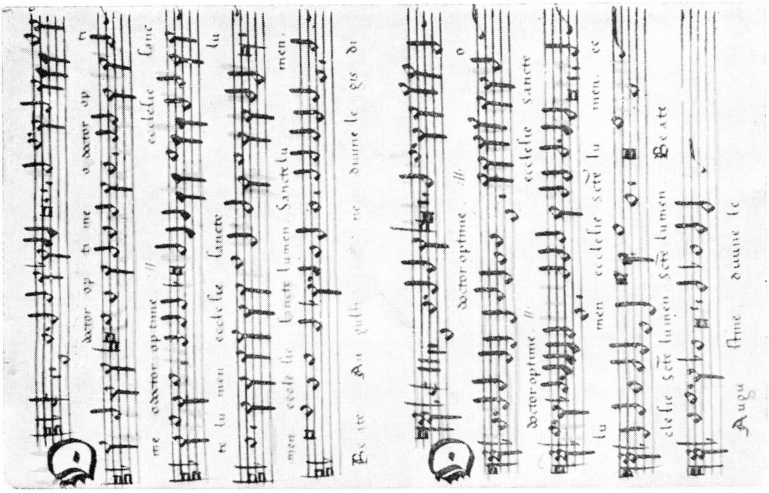

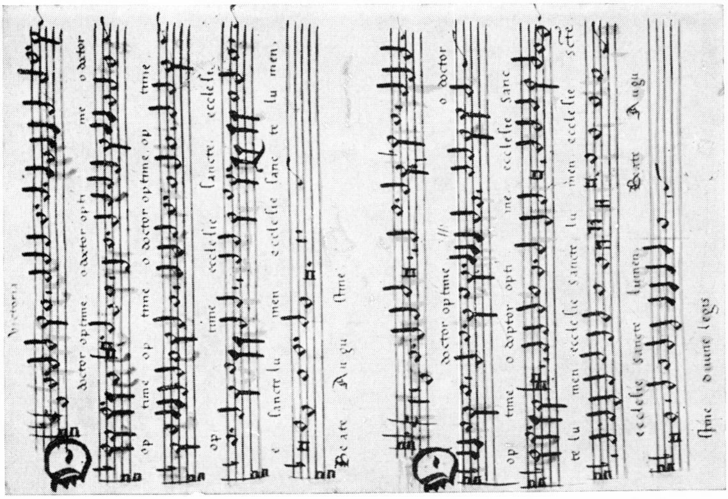

III

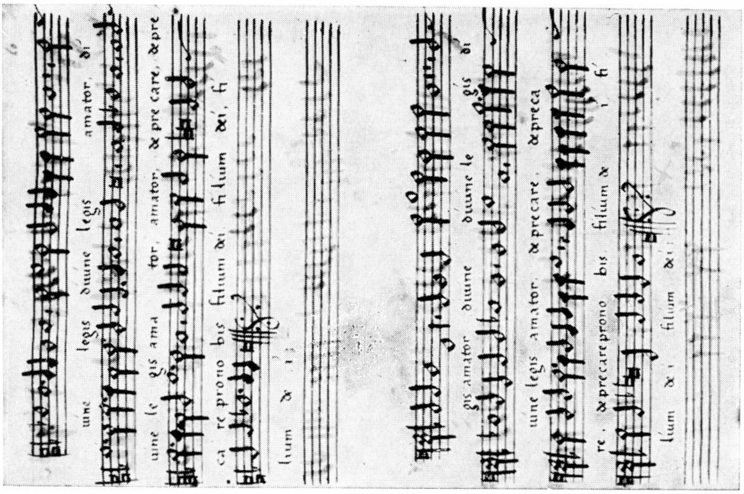

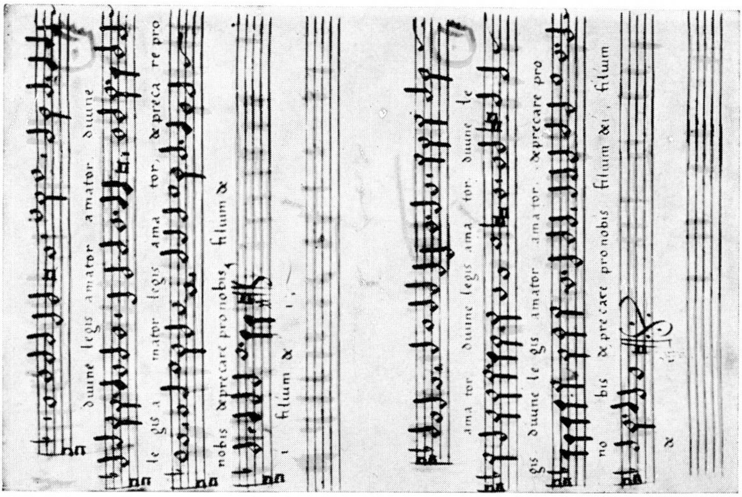

IV

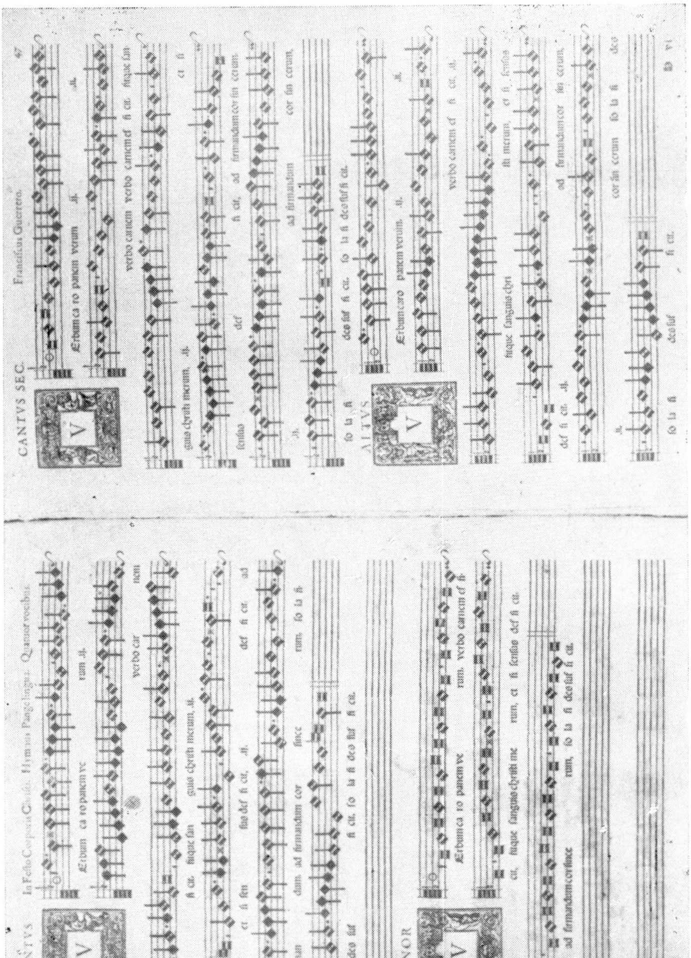
CANTVS
In Festo Corporis Christi. Hymnus Pange lingua. Quatuor vocibus.
TENOR
CANTVS SEC.
Franciscus Guerrero.
ALTVS

V

VI

VIII

IX

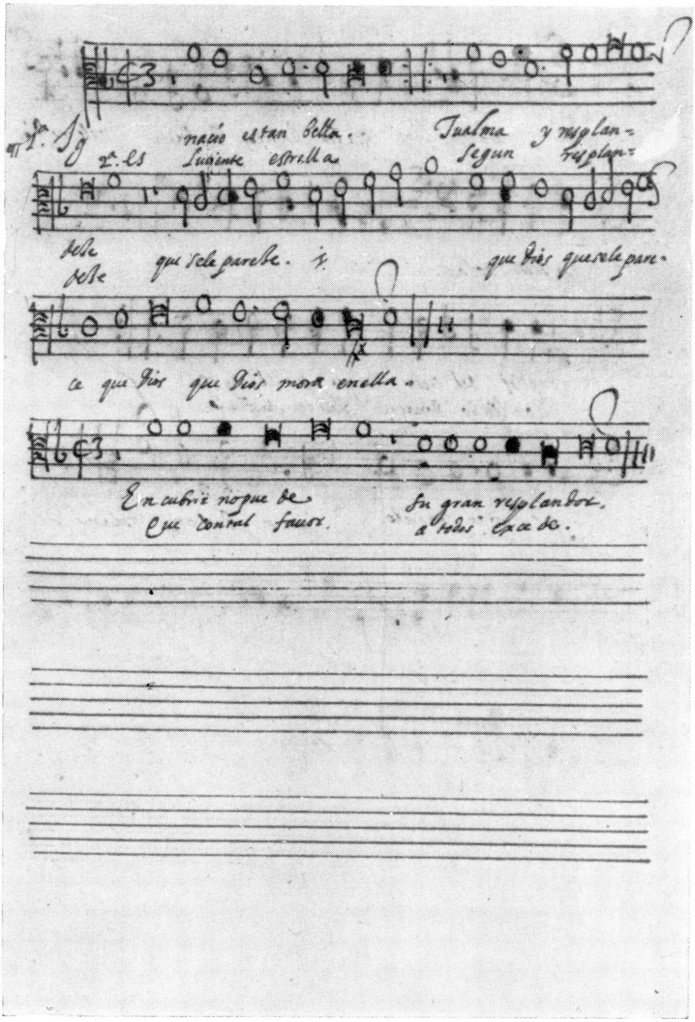

X

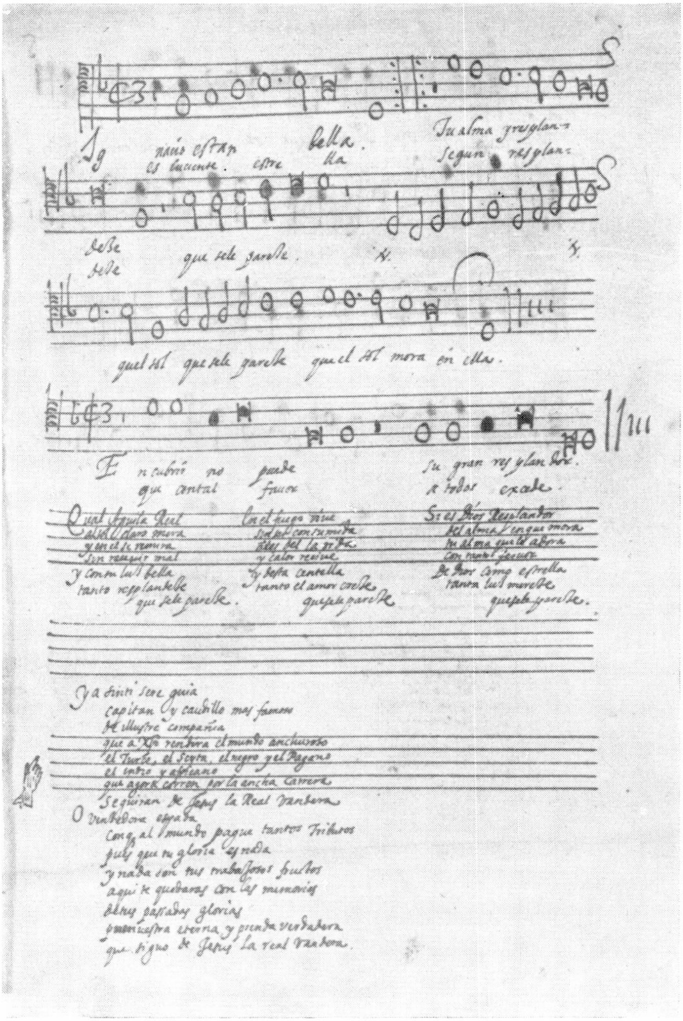

Agenda defunctorum.
Equiem e ter nam. O na
eis domine, & lux perpetua luceat eis
luceat eis. Te decet Himnus Deus in Sion.
Tti bi redetur votum in Hieru salem, exaudi ora tionem
meam, ad te omnis caro veniet.
O na eis do mine dona eis domine,
& lux perpetua luceat eis luceat
eis. luceat eis. T ti bi re
de tur votum in Hieru salem, in Hierusalem, exaudi ora
tionem meam, ad te omnis caro veniet.

XII

XIV

XV

XVI

Part I

Paleography

B

Various Conventions and Signs used in Writing

THE VOICES

In the composition and performance of their works the polyphonic composers of the sixteenth century used four kinds of vocal tone; *cantus* or *superius* (1) also described as a pure voice; *altus*, a young man's voice; *tenor*, a voice of medium range; and *bassus*, a deep voice.

The highest part was performed by boys from eight to twelve or thirteen years of age. Occasionally it was sung by men, in falsetto. (2)

On the other hand, the second part was never given to boys but to young tenors, whose range extended from F on the fourth line of the bass stave to A on the second space of the treble.

The tenor voice was the male voice *par excellence*. The whole composition normally revolves around his part.

To support the edifice of sound they depended on the man's deep voice, called for this reason *bassis* (3) in earlier times.

In compositions for more than four voices the composer doubles one of these voices depending on the requirements of the text and many other factors which might influence the choice of voices—inspiration, the number of singers available, etc.

THE DISPOSITION OF VOICES IN MANUSCRIPTS AND PRINTED EDITIONS

There were two procedures in use. Either they were written separately, each voice in a book, or all voices in the same book. In the latter case, wherever the book is opened, cantus and

tenor occupy the left-hand page, upper and lower half respectively, while altus and bassus are on the right, altus above and
bassus below. (4)

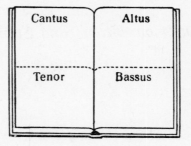

As voices were set out in this way, the singers could all read
from the same volume placed on a reading desk or lectern,
which explains the description 'libros de atril o de facistol'
(desk or lectern books) given to the large polyphonic manuscripts of the fifteenth, sixteenth and following centuries.

If the piece is for six voices, three are written on each page,
if for five, three on one and two on the other, or the first and
third on the left, the second and fourth on the right and the
fifth on staves below both, a hand or some other sign indicating
where the final stave of the first page finishes, and where that
voice continues below the part on the following page.

If the voices are written in separate books these are named
appropriately—*cantus* or *superius, altus, tenor* and *bassus*. Where
there are more than four the other books bear the names
quintus, sextus, septimus and *octavus*, according to whether there
are five, six, seven or eight voices. In these cases it should be
ascertained most carefully what sort of voice each part is
written for. Thus, for example, the fifth voice is not always a
tenor, as has been stated incorrectly. Sometimes it is a cantus,
sometimes one of the other voices.

If the piece is written for two cantus, altus, tenor, bassus, the
quintus will be cantus secundus; if for cantus, altus, two tenors
and bassus, it will be one of the two tenor parts. The same
considerations apply in the case of sextus, septimus and
octavus.

As a general rule, the voice required to perform it will be clearly shown at the top of each part. Where this is not done, it should be decided from the clefs.

THE CLEFS

To indicate the precise tessitura of each voice three clefs are used—G, C and F. The G clef, save for a few exceptions, is found only on the second line of the stave; the C clef on the first, second, third and fourth; the F clef on the third and fourth. (5)

The most commonly found disposition of clefs is shown in the following diagram:

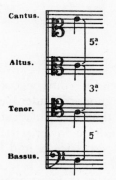

In this case the outer voices are separated from the middle voices by the interval of a fifth, and these themselves by that of a third.

In scores having a higher tessitura the clefs are set out thus: (6)

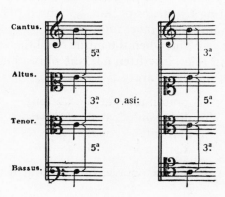

If the piece is for equal voices the grouping of clefs and the naming of the voices is usually one of these:

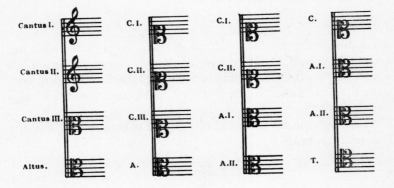

CANON

At the beginning or end of some pieces an asterisk, a cross, a sign which looks to the modern reader like a capital S, or a mark of interrogation with dots on either side is found, sometimes in an upper, sometimes in a lower part. The sign is an abbreviation for the Latin term *signum* and in textbooks is usually called *signum congruentiae.*

Its purpose is to show the point at which the second voice should begin in canon. (7) If the sign is found at the end of the piece, this shows where the imitation finishes, although the voices—at least one—may still have a short coda, some parts being closely connected with the last bars of the canon.

Composers do not always write out the answering voices, merely indicating by means of time-honoured phrases whether the interval is unison, octave, fifth, etc.

Both in this case and when the music of all the voices forming the canonic imitation is written out, the phrases used to specify the interval of imitation are:

> 'ad unisonum'   at the unison;
> 'in diapason'   at the octave;
> 'in diapente'   at the fifth;
> 'in diatesaron' at the fourth.

To indicate the upper octave, fifth or fourth the prefix *epi* or *hiper* is placed before the appropriate word. If the interval is lower they use the prefix *sub* or *hipo*. 'Canon in epidiapente' therefore means canon at the fifth higher, 'canon in subdiapente' canon at the fifth lower. (8)

If the answering voice is given, the term 'resolutio' is written at the beginning of it.

Apart from these phrases, others occur quite often at the beginning of a piece or at the beginning of the voice which states the theme. They constitute the key to the solution of what are called riddle canons, veritable jigsaw or musical crossword puzzles, very much to the taste of some poly-phonists of the fifteenth and sixteenth centuries. In many cases their realization and solution require a skill and effort worthy of a better cause.

THE DIRECT

This is a sign written at the end of each stave, showing the first note of the following stave. It takes many forms.

THE PAUSE

As at the present day this is found usually at the end of a piece. In transcription it appears in one of the following situations— at the end of one of the main divisions of a work, and at the end of the first half-versicle of psalm verses, provided that all voices join in a final cadence at this point. In the sixteenth century it indicated a suspension of movement—a definite pause at the end of a piece, and a temporary pause within a piece. In the latter case, says Zacconi, movement should be resumed before too long.

This sign was placed over long notes or over notes not less than a semibreve in duration.

Sometimes it was used above all the notes of a short piece to indicate a dignified, adagio style of performance, a necessary condition for this being that all the voices move homophonically, in chords. There is an example in *et homo factus est* of Antoine Brumel's mass *Fulgebunt justi*.

When the final chord of a piece carried a pause it could be prolonged almost indefinitely at the discretion of the singers. (9)

As a general rule the pause is found only in manuscripts. We cannot recall ever having seen it in printed music.

REPEAT MARKS

These generally consist of dots—sometimes two and sometimes four, one in each space of the stave. In pieces with Castilian text, comprising refrain and couplets, there are a great variety of signs at the end of the latter which indicate the repeat of the refrain.

The repetition of one or more words in the text is shown in printed music by two i's (ii), or an i and a j (ij). In manuscripts other signs are used, having the same meaning as those given above.

THE FLAT, SHARP AND NATURAL

The flat is the only sign of alteration used by the polyphonists as a key-signature. There is almost never more than one, so that if the note occurs twice within the stave the flat is shown again, quite logically, at the distance of an octave.

It is not uncommon to find pieces in which the flat as a key-signature is found in one voice only. (10)

In the remainder of the piece the flat is found only rarely. Sometimes it functions as a natural sign, that is to say it cancels out a previous sharp.

The sharp serves two purposes—sometimes to cancel out a flat, sometimes to raise the note a semitone. In the first case it is almost always placed before the note B, and in the second case before the notes C, F and G.

Where repeated notes occur, signs written before the first apply also to those following, but when a rest or another note comes between two or more statements of the same note, the sign written in front of the first sometimes concerns that alone, sometimes also those following.

The natural sign was rarely used in this period. At first it cancelled the flat while this cancelled the sharp, and it was not until the beginning of the eighteenth century that present-day usage became established.

Both in printed music and manuscripts—but more so in the latter—flat, sharp and natural are sometimes placed before the notes concerned, sometimes below or above them.

CHAPTER 2

The Notation of Polyphony

The musical notation of the sixteenth century represents a very advanced stage of development in the long evolutionary process which runs from polyphony's uncertain beginnings to its ice age. Its source or origin was the square Gregorian notation, in use from the beginning of the twelfth century, and it was, like this, black to begin with. The notes did not all appear at the same time; the four longest appeared first and were in general use by 1230, while the minim and crotchet came towards the end of the thirteenth century. The long and the breve derive respectively from the Gregorian *virga* and *punctum*, as ligatures do from neumes. It was as long ago as 1150, in the musical centres of Notre Dame de Paris, of St. Martial of Limoges and—like a reflection of the latter in Spain—Santiago de Compostela, that square Gregorian notation began to be used on lines, for the purpose of writing down the developing polyphony. About the year 1450 white notation began to replace black, except for notes shorter than a minim. These were still written in black, which continued to be used also to reduce the value of the longer ones. The reasons for this change were convenience, economy and above all because it led to better preservation of manuscripts, which were easily blurred by the large amount of black required by the longer notes. Until the end of the twelfth century music was written in score. After this the practice was discontinued, except for the conductus which was still so written in the thirteenth century. During these centuries and up to the sixteenth century eminent authorities made progressive attempts to simplify the extremely complicated notation of this period.

In this worthy task Spain played a very important part.

With the rise of printing this simplification proceeded with greater speed, as it was impossible to reproduce in print all the finer points of manuscript. This was how matters stood about

the year 1550. It was Ottaviano dei Petrucci, an Italian born in
Fossombrone, who began in 1501 to print polyphonic music,
using metal types in double rows, a practice which was rather
too costly, although it maintained a balance between perfection,
beauty and accuracy. More practical was the method of the
Frenchman Pierre Haultin—introduced in 1525—which was
capable of printing both notes and text with a single line of
type. Pierre Attaignant made use of it in his collections of
organ music. Briard—about 1532—tried without success to
change the rhomboid type of notes to round ones, as used by
copyists from much earlier times. The rhomboid shape persists,
in some editions, well into the eighteenth century. Printing
did not succeed in solving the problem of scores, each voice part
being printed in a separate book, or all the voice parts in large
volumes as in desk (or lectern) manuscripts. The development of printed Spanish music has yet to be studied. The oldest
editions were made in Salamanca in the years 1492, 1498 and
1504. Some treatises of this period show the staves without
notation which would have to be written by hand. The first
editions of polyphonic music printed in Spain are the *Villancicos
y canciones* of Juan Vásquez (Osuna, 1551) and his *Agenda
defunctorum* (Seville, 1556).

THE NOTES AND RESTS

The theorists used the word *figura* to indicate two groups of
signs—notes and rests. (1)

The former are described as *figuras cantables*, the latter as
figuras incantables. (2)

The *figuras cantables* used in the sixteenth century are eight in
number—*large, long, breve, semibreve, minim, crotchet, quaver* and
semiquaver, in descending order of magnitude.

Maxima Longa Breve Semibreve Minima Semiminima   Corchea   Semicorchea.

The quaver and semiquaver sometimes appear in the form
shown in parentheses, especially in the manuscript music of the
last years of the sixteenth and the first years of the seventeenth
centuries.

Each note has a corresponding rest:

NOTE-VALUES

Note-values are considered from two standpoints—their relation to each other and their relation to the length of the bar.

NOTE-VALUES IN RELATION TO EACH OTHER

The theorists distinguish between four relationships—that of large to long, long to breve, breve to semibreve and semibreve to minim.

(i) The relationship between large and long—*Greater Mood*.

The relationship between large and long and between long and breve is known as *Mood*.

In the first case it is Greater Mood, classified as perfect or imperfect according to whether the large is equivalent to three or two longs.

(ii) The relationship between long and breve—*Lesser Mood*.

This is divided similarly into perfect and imperfect. In the first case the long equals three breves and in the second case two.

The method of indicating Mood is not the same with all authors. Some show it 'by a combination of numbers, circles and semicircles', (3) that is, by writing at the beginning of the piece a circle or semicircle followed by one or more numbers, for example: 033, 03, 032, 02. The first figure refers to Mood, the second to Time and the third—if there is a third—to Prolation. (See below.)

Others show it by means of three vertical lines, stretching across three spaces on the stave to indicate perfect relationship and across two when this is imperfect. (4)

The same device is used to indicate Lesser Mood, the only difference being that instead of three vertical lines there are only two.

These lines were generally written between the clef and the time-signature, to distinguish them from the rests which sometimes follow at the beginnings of the voice parts. (5)

Although the theorists still spoke of mood its practice had fallen into abeyance by the sixteenth century.

(iii) The relationship between breve and semibreve—*Time*.

As with mood, Time was divided into perfect and imperfect. In the former, the value of the breve is three semibreves, in the latter, two.

Time Perfect is shown by means of a circle, Time Imperfect by a semicircle.

The sign of Time, especially that of Time Imperfect, is the one most used throughout the sixteenth century.

(iv) The relationship between semibreve and minim—*Prolation*.

Prolation means the division of the semibreve, ternary or binary according to whether Prolation is perfect or imperfect. If perfect, the semibreve equals three minims, when imperfect, two.

A dot within the circle or semicircle always indicates Prolation Perfect. The absence of the dot indicates Prolation Imperfect.

The relationship between the lesser note-values is always binary.

The combination of Time and Prolation occurs in four different ways expressed by the following Latin phrases:

In the first case the division of notes is always binary, each note equalling two of its immediate inferior;

In the second case the division of the breve is ternary, but of the other notes binary;

In the third case the division of the breve is binary, that of the semibreve ternary and of the others binary again;

In the fourth case the division of breve and semibreve is ternary, but of those less than the semibreve, binary.

CHAPTER 3

Note-Values in Relation
to the Bar

Just as it is useless nowadays knowing that a semibreve equals two minims, a minim two crotchets, a dotted crotchet three quavers, and so on, without knowing also the number and type of notes comprising the bar, so it is little use understanding the theory of Mood, Time and Prolation if we do not understand the constitution of the bar represented by its respective time-signatures and the distribution of the notes in each of its parts.

Two questions arise in connection with this problem. What types of bar were known and used by the polyphonists? What notes, and how many of them, were found in each bar and in its various parts?

THE BARS IN USE DURING THE SIXTEENTH CENTURY

To appreciate the scope of this question more fully, it should be borne in mind that during the greater part of the last three hundred years we have used only three types of bar, one of two beats, another of three beats and a third of four.

Was the situation different in the sixteenth century? Did they, in contrast to present-day procedure, recognize only one of these bars?

The only real uncertainty concerns the ternary bar, since it is quite clear that the polyphonists did not know the four-beat bar and that the two-beat bar was in everyday use.

With regard to the ternary bar, it is generally accepted that this is what is indicated by the complete circle, by the broken circle followed by the number 3, and by various other signs.

Nevertheless, its existence has been called in question by the Italian musicologist Tirabassi (1) whose theories are disseminated and enthusiastically defended by Antoine Auda. (2)

Tirabassi holds that the bar was invariably composed of two

equal beats, a uniform movement of the hand down and up. Sometimes two, sometimes three notes were performed within the time of those beats.

This is the same as saying today that the 2/4 and 3/4 bars are made up of two equal beats, but with two crotchets in the 2/4 bar and three in the 3/4.

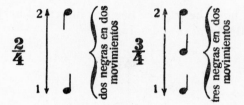

What is the answer to this problem?

After detailed study of the question we have reached the following conclusions. We consider Tirabassi's theories about the ternary bar to be incorrect, but we agree with him concerning the binary interpretation of the sign of Time Perfect.

THE EXISTENCE OF THE TERNARY BAR IN THE SIXTEENTH CENTURY

Here is the evidence of various theorists:

> There are two different types of bar in practical music. In one the bar (as is commonly said) is divided into two equal parts, and in the other into three parts, also equal. The latter is the bar whose proportion is described as ternary, in which two of its three parts take place on the downward movement and one on the upward movement. . . . This has two semibreves or two minims sung to the downward movement and one to the upward. . . . (3)

From this is it obvious that the bar was not invariably composed—as Tirabassi would have it—of two beats of the same duration over which sometimes two and sometimes three notes were spread, but that in some cases it was made up of three equal or two unequal movements, the first being twice the length of the second, two semibreves being sung to the former and one to the latter.

> Although all parts of the three divisions of the ternary bar are equal to one another, the bar is nevertheless not symmetrical but

non-symmetrical, the downbeat being twice the length of the upbeat, two of the three divisions being sung during the downward movement and one during the upward movement— one, two on the downbeat, three on the upbeat. I assert that the first comes on the downbeat of the bar, the second is sung within the same period or passage of time and the third on the upbeat, as stated in the sixth book of the present treatise. (4)

We show how the ternary bar was indicated in the sixteenth century in the form of a diagram:

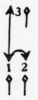

This is confirmed by the extremely reputable theorists Montanos and Llorente, among others. The first of these puts it this way:

> The bar of ternary division or proportion (as it is called by others) having three notes in a bar, is not divided into two equal parts, that is, into downbeat and upbeat like the normal binary bar, but the first note is on the downbeat, then the second note is sung, and the third comes on the upbeat. (5)

Andrés Llorente expresses himself in almost identical terms. (6)

But Spanish theorists are not the only ones to affirm the existence of the ternary or non-symmetrical bar; many non-Spanish theorists are also of the same opinion. In his monumental treatise Zacconi writes:

> In writing my Prattica di Musica I would have been quite prepared to proceed immediately to consideration of the notes, if I had not by chance found something which disagrees in detail with the view generally held. I maintain that there may be one simple bar, namely the symmetrical bar, the reason being that the ancients in their proportions did not use any other: but that it became corrupted, little by little, to suit the convenience of singers and not because of necessity or reason. I have assumed that

it would be possible for others also to see the matter in this light, and share the same point of view, and that it will be as well to discuss the divisions of the bar and the strength of these divisions: so that because of what I say everyone may be convinced and rest content with the truth. (7)

Zacconi devotes a long chapter to proving the practice of the non-symmetrical bar, stressing the same idea in various other places.

To sum up, in the sixteenth century two types of bar were in use: binary, comprising two movements, and ternary, having three.

There were two ways of indicating the ternary bar—one of three equal beats and the other of two unequal beats, the first being twice the duration of the second.

CHAPTER 4

The Number of Notes
in Each Bar and in
Each of its Parts

THE SIGN OF TIME IMPERFECT: C

The binary bar is indicated by the sign of Time Imperfect, the semicircle C. (It was known in Spain as *compasillo* and *compasete*.)

The unit of the bar is the semibreve, or its equivalent, two minims (one in each part), four crotchets (two in each part), and so on. The longer notes are twice the value of those immediately less in length—the breve, two semibreves (or two bars)—the long, two breves—the large, two longs.

If the semicircle is divided by a vertical stroke, this indicates that the bar contained twice the number of notes. The total value in this case is the breve, or, what amounts to the same thing, each part of the bar may contain a semibreve, two minims, four crotchets, eight quavers or sixteen semiquavers.

This bar is also indicated by the semicircle followed by the number 2, or by the semicircle reversed.

(In Spain it was called *compás mayor*.)

Transcription exercise. Plates I–III.
Practical suggestions:

1. Modern musicologists do not agree concerning what sort of bar should be chosen for transcribing music written with the sign of Time Imperfect, in the sixteenth century.

Since this corresponds to a binary bar, it is possible to choose any one of these, 1/1, 2/4, 2/1 (alla breve). Strictly speaking, it is possible also to choose our 2/2 bar. We prefer this because it gives the most room between the bar lines.

The important thing in each case is to seek an exact correspondence between the values of the original and the modern
notations, so that the note representing one part of the bar in
the original should be given its equivalent in the transcription:
the equivalent of two should be transcribed as two, and
so on.

2. There is also some difference of opinion concerning the
reduction of note-values. While the musicologists of the early
part of the century (Karl Proske, H. Bellerman, F. X.
Haberl, Adolf Sandberger, Theodor Kroyer, Johannes Wolf,
Knud Jeppesen) preferred notes of long duration, the tendency
today is towards the opposite extreme, even to the point of
reducing them to a quarter of their size (Hugo Riemann—
who began this trend—Willi Apel, Heinrich Besseler). Between
these two extremes there is a half-way house, in which the note-
values are reduced by a half.

3. Contrary to what was accepted procedure until quite
recently, today all voices are written in the G clef with the
exception of the bass, which always has the F clef sign on the
fourth line. If the altus part is set very low it is written an
octave higher, a number 8 given below the clef indicating that
it should be sung an octave lower than it is written. This is
standard procedure with the tenor voice.

4. The original clef of each voice part should be shown at
the beginning of the piece, as should also the time-signature
and the shape (*figura*) of the first note. In this way the reader
can satisfy himself completely that the signs chosen by the
transcriber are equivalent to those of the original.

5. The distinction between Time Imperfect with the original
note-values and with the note-values reduced is a matter of
theory rather than practice, particularly in the second half
of the sixteenth century. It was customary to use the latter,
but with the note-values appropriate to the first, the breve
being equivalent to two bars, the semibreve to one and so on.
Various authors confirm this view. (1)

6. The dot written to the right of a note means the same as
it does today, and is accordingly called the dot of augmentation.
(The other two—extremely rare in this period—will be dealt
with later.)

7. The breve and semibreve are sometimes written in black.

If so, they lose a quarter of their value. If they are half white and half black they lose an eighth.

8. To determine the value of ligatures refer to Chapter 5.

THE SIGN OF TIME PERFECT: O

As we have already seen, the circle is the sign of Time Perfect, and indicates the ternary division of the breve. Because of this it has traditionally been understood to be a ternary bar. Tirabassi was the first to assert that this interpretation was incorrect, claiming that the circle represents a binary bar, despite the fact that following this sign the breve was equivalent to and can be divided into three semibreves.

We agree with this theory.

According to the Renaissance theorists the breve was equal to three semibreves in Time Perfect. This can be interpreted in two ways, namely, that Time Perfect means a bar divided into three parts, a semibreve to each part, this being the traditional interpretation—or that Time Perfect means a bar divided into two parts, with each of the three semibreves into which the breve is divided constituting a bar in its own right. In the first interpretation the three semibreves into which the breve is divided are sung within one bar; in the second they extend over three bars. In the first they are sung as only three parts of a bar, to three movements of the hand; while in the second six parts or movements of the hand are required for their performance.

As can be appreciated with the following example, there is a tremendous difference between the two interpretations.

The traditional interpretation is as follows:

While Tirabassi's is like this:

Which is correct? In our opinion it is the second. But what do the theorists have to say?

In his *Arte tripharia*, Bermudo writes:

There is a time called perfect, which is indicated thus: O.

Sometimes this has a dot in the centre and is called half Time Perfect. In the first case the large equals twelve bars, the long six, the breve three and the semibreve one. There are two minims in a bar, four crotchets in a bar, eight quavers in a bar and sixteen semiquavers in a bar. (2)

Accordingly, after the sign of Time Perfect the breve equals three bars and not three parts of a bar, and as the semibreve equals one bar, and two minims equal one, and so on, it follows that it implies a binary bar and not a ternary one at all.

The same thing, illustrated by the example given below, is affirmed by Montanos:

In Time Perfect the notes have the following values:

That is to say the large equals twelve bars, the long six, the breve three, the semibreve one and the minim a half.

Here is the testimony of a non-Spanish author:

And so the system of organization in any piece of music must be deduced from the sign which precedes it. For if this implies ternary organization, that is, perfection of time . . . we shall use separate semibreves in separate bars. Indeed this procedure is so obvious, that no one by whom this matter has been investigated will not be aware of it. Accordingly we use two minims to the bar or (in other words) four crotchets. (3)

The text is clear—it is speaking of Time Perfect within which 'separate semibreves are performed as separate bars', that is to say, one semibreve to the bar.

So that we shall not misunderstand this nor any other text using the word 'tactus', we must realize that this word has the same meaning as 'compás' (= bar) and that it should never be regarded as equal to one of its parts.

We shall end discussion of this subject with some words of Zacconi:

. . . *All songs of time perfect and imperfect are sung with the symmetrical* (*bar*) and all proportions and natural prolation with the non-symmetrical bar. *The songs of time perfect,* as well as those of time imperfect indicated by a plain semicircle *are sung with one semibreve to the bar*, the perfections falling into place quite naturally. Accordingly, those songs with the divided semicircle are sung with one breve to the bar. (4)

The unbroken circle can be divided by a vertical line or accompanied by the number 2. In both cases 'the notes and rests lose half their value'. (5)

Summing up, the unbroken as well as the broken circle indicates a binary bar, the unit of the bar being a semibreve. The basic difference between the two bars is that in the first the breve, in order to be perfect, equals three semibreves, or, what amounts to the same thing, three bars; while in the second the breve equals only two semibreves, and, accordingly, two bars.

The following examples will make our explanations plainer:

(1) Note-values in Time Imperfect, C:

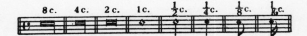

Transcription:

(2) Note-values in half Time Imperfect:

Transcription:

(3) Note-values in Time Perfect O:

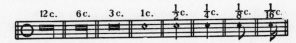

(4) Note-values in half Time Perfect:

Transcription:

Transcription exercise. Plate IV.

Remarks:

1. Guerrero's *Pange lingua* is written with the sign of Time Perfect using the original note-values. It should be transcribed twice, according both to our theory and to traditional procedure. In the first case a binary bar will be chosen, giving each semibreve of the original its full value. In the second a ternary bar should be used and each semibreve given half its value.

2. In both cases it must be remembered that when a number of breves occur in succession,

    (*a*) each one of them except the last is perfect, that is, equivalent to three semibreves;

    (*b*) the last is perfect if followed by a rest of its own or greater value—otherwise it is imperfect.

3. The perfect breve loses one third of its value when it is completely black, and one sixth if it is half-black and half-white.

4. If two semibreves appear between two breves it must be borne in mind

    that the two breves are perfect;

    that the second semibreve doubles its value ('es alterada' according to the theorists); but

    that if between the two semibreves (in the upper or the

lower part) there is a dot (*punctum divissionis*), then the two breves are imperfect and the second semibreve has its usual value; that is to say, the two breves are imperfect, the first because of the semibreve which follows it, the second because of the semibreve that precedes it (6) 'imperfectio a parte poste e imperfectio a parte ante'.

PROLATION

Both the sign of Time Perfect and that of Time Imperfect can have a dot in the centre.

In both cases this is called Prolation Perfect, as opposed to Imperfect, which is indicated by the absence of the dot. (7)

Prolation is the measure of capacity of the semibreve, as is Greater Mood of the large, Lesser Mood of the long and Time of the breve.

In Times with Prolation the semibreve acquires the characteristics proper to the breve in Time Perfect. The semibreve accordingly is equal to three minims when it is perfect, that is, whenever it is followed by another semibreve or by a rest of its own or greater value.

Prolation was invented to extend the length of the notes.

> Prolation was placed in music for the lengthening of notes and rests, this being what is meant by *Prolatio, prolationis*. And, therefore, in times with Prolation, notes and rests have much greater value than in those without it. (8)

The interpretation of this sign is a difficult problem, being aggravated by the difference of opinion prevailing among sixteenth-century authors themselves. While some say it is a binary bar others say that it implies a ternary bar.

Llorente writes: 'In those Times with Prolation, the minim equals one bar and the semibreve three when it has no number in front of it.' (9) In the *tabla del valor de las figuras* he points out that in Prolation, the bar is regarded as binary both in Time Perfect and Time Imperfect. (10)

According to this the semibreve has the value of or is equivalent to three binary bars, and the minim is equal to one. Two crotchets may constitute a bar, and four quavers or eight semiquavers likewise.

Here are the values of all these notes:

Time Perfect with Prolation:

Its modern equivalent:

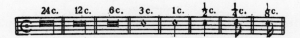

Time Imperfect with Prolation:

Its modern equivalent:

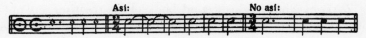

The distinction between the two times lies in the differing values of the longer notes.

According to this theory, the duration of the semibreve is equal to three binary bars and not to three parts of a ternary bar:

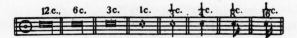

From the table of values given by Bermudo in his *Declaración de instrumentos musicales* (11) it appears that he also regards Prolation as indicating a binary bar, but with an important difference in the interpretation of note-values.

Time Perfect with Prolation:

ERRATUM (*Page 25*)

The second example is incorrect and should in fact be identical with the fourth example.

Its equivalent:

Time Imperfect with Prolation:

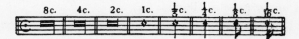

Its equivalent:

Obviously in these examples he is postulating a binary bar, composed of four crotchets.

Traditionally, both signs have been interpreted as signifying a ternary bar, a practice whose only connection with the facts of the situation is the ternary division of the semibreve, although, as we have pointed out in dealing with Time Perfect, a note can be divided into three without this necessitating a ternary bar.

If the ternary bar is used, these are the comparative note-values:

In support of this usage it is possible to adduce the authority of Zacconi who, in the second book of his treatise, sets out to prove how Prolation should be measured by the non-symmetrical bar. (12)

This has already been affirmed by the author in the text quoted in this chapter dealing with Time Perfect.

However, in the *tabla del valor de las figuras* given on page 131v. of his treatise he assigns to the notes of Times with Prolation a value equal to that given by Tapia, Llorente and other authors.

The interpretation given to the sign of Prolation by Tirabassi and Auda should be given special mention. According to these authors, the unit of value, as opposed to the situations found in the systems of Greater Mood, Lesser Mood and Time, is double in Prolation—the semibreve when all the voices bear the sign of Prolation, and the minim when it is borne by only one. Keeping to their theory of the non-existence of the ternary bar, they interpret Prolation as a binary procedure. In the first case the perfect semibreve equals a bar and the minim one third of a bar, while in the second the notes increase their value, the semibreve being equal to three bars and the minim to one. (Auda: 'La prolation dans l'édition princeps de la messe "L'homme armé" de Palestrina et sa resolution dans l'édition de 1599'—*Scriptorium*, 1948, Vol. II, pp. 85–102.)

As well as the many cogent arguments cited by Tirabassi and Auda in support of their view it is possible to bring forward that of Bermudo:

> If a dot is placed within the time-signature in all the voices it signifies Prolation Perfect and makes the semibreve perfect. I say in all the voices, because its appearance in one would not indicate Prolation but augmentation. In Prolation a bar equals three minims and in augmentation one. (13)

To these interpretations we should add the one given by Apel, comparing Time Perfect and Imperfect with a bar of 9/8 and 6/8 respectively. (Apel: *The notation of polyphonic music, 900–1600*, Cambridge, Mass., 1949, pp. 98, 120–3.)

Which of these theories corresponds to the facts of history? The answer needs more space than is available in an elementary textbook.

Without going so far as to examine in detail each of the opinions expressed, we can say we prefer that of Tirabassi. (Our reasons will be the theme of an extensive study which we are planning on this topic.)

In relation to practice, the main concern of this book, it seems fitting to warn the reader of the relatively minor importance of this question, since in the sixteenth century few pieces were written using the sign of Prolation. Some polyphonists, Victoria, for example, do not use it at all. Some use it only in combination with other mensural signs. In collections such as the *Cancionero de la Casa de Medinaceli* or the *Cancionero musical de los siglos XV y XVI* of Barbieri, containing 100 and 250 pieces respectively, it appears only rarely.

CHAPTER 5

The Proportions

Proportion was defined by Johannes de Muris as the comparison between two numbers or two symbols. (1)

Number one compared with numbers two, three and four; two compared with three; six with four, etc., are the kinds of proportion which had a practical application in musical composition from the fourteenth to the sixteenth centuries.

It sometimes happens that while one voice has so many notes within a bar, such as three semibreves, another voice performs, within the same space of time, a different number of notes of the same type—say, two semibreves—thus automatically producing numerical comparison or proportion.

The theory of proportion, with its unusual terminology, its classifications, the varieties of each kind and many other ramifications, constitutes a puzzle of very little practical use for us; moreover possibly only half a dozen were used by any one composer of the period.

We shall therefore limit ourselves to dealing only with those found most frequently—almost exclusively—in compositions of the sixteenth century. (2)

Proportions are indicated by precise signs formed almost always by two numbers, one over the other.

These signs sometimes accompany time-signatures, changing their meaning. At other times they are found on their own, and this is when the real nature of proportion becomes evident. The two questions will be discussed separately.

THE SIGNS OF TIME PERFECT AND IMPERFECT
ACCOMPANIED BY PROPORTIONAL NUMBERS

Time signatures can be accompanied by the number 2, in which case the notes have the same value as when the same signs are divided by a vertical stroke.

Time-signatures—divided or undivided—are sometimes seen

to be modified by the number 3. This is explained as follows: 'If the number three is used it means that three notes are to be sung in a bar normally containing two, the notes being of the same kind in each case, and it is called triple or sesquialtera proportion. . . .' (3)

So if we are dealing with the undivided time-signature accompanied by the number 3 we have a ternary bar, a minim being sung in each one of its parts, the bar comprising a perfect semibreve; while if the sign is divided the bar is made up of three semibreves, one in each division of the bar.

But 2 and 3 are incomplete forms of the proportions 2/1, 3/1, 3/2. The third of these is frequently found in company with the divided circle. (4)

When dealing with Time Perfect we must remember what was said in the previous chapter about the perfection of the breve when it precedes another breve, or a rest of its own or longer duration, and also concerning the alteration of the semibreves.

Transcription exercise. Plates V–VII.

Essential instructions: In the pieces written with divided time-signature and accompanied by the proportion 3/2,

(*a*) Breve and semibreve are frequently black in colour. Their value is the same as if they were white;

(*b*) Some composers give the same value to crotchet and minim after this sign;

(*c*) The quaver is frequently coloured white.

Special attention should be given to works where the sign of Time Imperfect is accompanied by the number 3 in printed editions, and similarly to a 3 or a 2 used at different times in manuscripts.

Within this bar the semibreve and minim and their respective rests acquire the properties of the breve and the semibreve in Time Perfect.

Transcription exercise. Plates VIII–X.

Remarks:

1. This composition should be transcribed on the basis of any

exact correspondence between the note-values of the manuscript and the transcription. Quartering the original note-values (i.e. using the 3/4 time-signature) is recommended, as it gives the most accurate idea of appropriate tempo in performance.

2. Black breves and semibreves appear at the same point in all three parts. Their value will be the same as if they were white.

3. An instance of parallel movement in octaves will be found in bar 6. A suitable suggestion for alteration in the appropriate part should be made in the course of the transcription. Other unexpected combinations of part-movement will be found, but these do not require alteration.

4. In the last phrase of the composition there occurs a discrepancy of a different kind. This should be corrected.

5. As in all transcription exercises, indicate where chromatic alteration may possibly have been used in performance. (Such suggestions can be checked against information given in Chapters 7–9, inclusive.)

PROPORTIONAL SIGNS BY THEMSELVES

It should be emphasized that proportions are indicated by precise signs, usually composed of two numbers, the upper indicating the number of notes in the bar, and the lower the type of note.

The most important are the *dupla* 2/1, the *tripla* 3/1, and the *sesquialtera* 3/2.

The dupla indicates that one voice sings two semibreves to another's one—the tripla and sesquialtera, that while one voice sings three semibreves or three minims another sings two.

These proportions are matched by others in which the numbers are inverted, this inversion denoting a meaning precisely the opposite to the original. They are designated by the same terms preceded by the prefix *sub*: *subdupla*, *subtripla*, *subsesquialtera*, and shown thus: 1/2, 1/3, 2/3.

Comparing the two types, it is obvious that while the former causes a genuine diminution of note-values, the second augments them. Thus, in dupla, tripla and sesquialtera proportions the notes in the part concerned diminish their value, according to the fraction formed by the numbers, that is to say, they lose a half, a third, etc. But in the subdupla, subtripla and subsesquialtera proportions the notes increase their value according to the fraction indicated by the signs: a half, a third, etc.

Because of this, the second type was used appropriately to revoke the effect of the first, this being done when it was desired to cancel the effect of the dupla, tripla or sesquialtera. Thus, 1/2 was cancelled out by 2/1, 2/3 by 3/2. The presence of the proportions indicated by the prefix *sub* indicates the return of normal note-values, which can also be indicated by the sign of Time Imperfect:

Apart from the proportions just explained—and many others not used as much as these—we should mention one which appears without any sign to indicate its presence.

This proportion, called *hemiolia*, belongs quite definitely to the same group as the sesquialtera. It is found in passages composed of white notes within which there appears a long succession of black notes, changed to imperfect by their colour.

In the hemiolia, greater or lesser according to whether it is formed of breves and semibreves, or of semibreves and minims, a group of three notes is placed over against two of the same type. It is not necessary to distinguish it by means of special signs, since the series of black notes makes its presence obvious.

From all that has been said about proportions it will be clear that their purpose was, simply, to augment or diminish the note-values in one part when required, while the other parts follow the pattern of procedure determined by the time-signature given at the beginning of the piece.

Thus, a sign of proportion appearing by itself is much more likely to be found during the course of a piece than at its beginning.

LIGATURES (5)

The name of ligature is given to groups of two or more notes joined together in writing. Some theorists call them *neumes*, because of their similarity to the Gregorian neumes from which they originate.

Three main things must be taken into account in dealing with ligatures—the ascending or descending stem attached to the first note; square notes shaped like breves; and oblique notes derived from the Gregorian porrectus and known in Spain as *alfas*.

Ligatures can be ascending or descending both at the beginning and the end. They are ascending at the beginning when the second note is higher than the first, even if the remaining notes are lower. They are always ascending at the end when the final note is higher than the one preceding it.

They are descending at the beginning when the second note is lower than the first, even if the following notes are higher. They are descending at the end, if the final note is lower than the one preceding it.

The whole secret in dealing with ligatures lies in knowing which notes are longs, which breves and which semibreves. The general rule is 'omnis media brevis', which means that in each ligature of more than two notes, all those between the first and the last are breves.

It remains only to determine the values of these—an easy matter, as the following examples show: (6)

1. *Ligatures with the stem extending downwards*

(*a*) Descending at the beginning and at the end. The first note is a breve. The last is a long if it is square in shape, a breve if it is oblique.

(*b*) Descending at the beginning, ascending at the end. The first and last notes are breves.

2. *Ligatures with the stem extending upwards*

(*a*) Ascending or descending at the beginning, ascending at the end. The first and second notes (by way of exception to the general rule) are semibreves, and the last is a breve. But if there are only two notes, both are semibreves.

(*b*) Ascending or descending at the beginning, descending at the end. The first and second notes are semibreves and the last is a long, but if there are only two notes, both are semibreves.

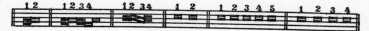

3. *Ligatures without a stem*

(*a*) Ascending at beginning and end. The first and last notes are breves.

(*b*) Ascending at the beginning, descending at the end. The first note is a breve and the last a long—but if the last is oblique in shape, it is a breve.

(*c*) Descending at the beginning and the end. The first and last notes are longs.

D

(*d*) Descending at the beginning and ascending at the end. The first note is a long and the last is a breve.

(*d*) Descending at the beginning and ascending at the end. The first note is a long and the last is a breve.

4. *Oblique shapes*
    (*a*) With stem ascending. Both notes are semibreves.
    (*b*) With stem descending. Both notes are breves.
    (*c*) Without a stem. The first is a long and the second, a breve.

Transcription exercise. Plates XI–XVI.

CHAPTER 6

Modality

The works of the sixteenth-century polyphonists—especially the early ones—were composed, more in theory than in practice, on the basis of the Gregorian modes, *protus*, *deuterus*, *tritus* and *tetrardus*, which, divided into authentic and plagal, gave rise to the eight classical modes. (1) (In Spain the authentic modes were given the name *maestros*, the plagal modes, *discípulos*.)

The finals of these modes are, of course, the notes D, E, F and G: D for the first and second, E for the third and fourth, F for the fifth and sixth, and G for the seventh and eighth.

In spite of their common final, the authentic mode differed from its corresponding plagal mode in having a different dominant, because of the position of the final in relation to the other notes of the scale, and because of its disposition and extension. While in the authentic modes the final is found at the extremes of the scale, in the plagal modes it is at the centre.

The scale of the authentic modes consists of an octave in ascending order from the final. This octave was divided into two parts, the first formed by a fifth—the pentachord—and the second by a fourth—the tetrachord.

In the authentic modes the pentachord consists of the lower part of the scale and the tetrachord of the upper. In the plagal modes, on the other hand, the tetrachord occupies the lower part and the pentachord the upper.

If the tetrachord of the first mode is transferred to the lower octave, the scale corresponding to the second mode is obtained.

By applying this same procedure to each one of the four authentic modes, the corresponding plagal modes are obtained.

SYSTEMATIC TABLE OF THE EIGHT MODES

Mode			Scale	Dom.	Final
1	Protus	Authentic. Dorian.	D–A–D	A	D
2		Plagal. Hypodorian.	A–D–A	F	D
3	Deuterus	Authentic. Phrygian.	E–B–E	C	E
4		Plagal. Hypophrygian.	B–E–B	A	E
5	Tritus	Authentic. Lydian.	F–C–F	C	F
6		Plagal. Hypolydian.	C–F–C	A	F
7	Tetrardus	Authentic. Mixolydian.	G–D–G	D	G
8		Plagal. Hypomixolydian.	D–G–D	C	G

To the eight notes of each scale the polyphonists added 'two permitted alterations, in one case the flattening of a note, in the other the sharpening of a note'. (2) This procedure arises out of the impossibility of forming cadences without the assistance of these altered notes, as will become obvious in discussion of the *semitonia subintellecta*.

As a general rule the first and second modes are written not with D but with G as their final, their scales accordingly appearing as follows, *with B flat present as a key-signature.*

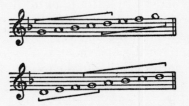

The other modes are written in their appropriate diatonic form. It should be noted, however, that the polyphonists nearly always write modes five and six with B flat as a key-signature, for one of the following reasons: in order to avoid the tritone (which occurs between B natural and the final in both cases); because of the impossibility of forming the major triad on the fourth degree while it remains B natural; and above all (especially with the fifth mode) because of the ascendancy (due to the evolutionary process of modality) that the major mode acquires in this period. (3)

To decide whether a polyphonic piece is in an authentic or its corresponding plagal mode all that is needed is to examine the highest part 'which so governs all the other voices, that they do not stray outside the confines and limits of the mode'. (4)

If the highest voice lies between the final and its upper octave the piece is in an authentic mode. If it ranges from the final to a fifth above and a fourth below it is plagal.

It should be pointed out, at the same time, that in a large proportion of cases it is not possible to state definitely whether a piece is in the authentic or plagal mode, since the highest voice includes the whole, or almost the whole of the range of both scales, thus producing a natural merging of the two modes.

RULES FOR DETERMINING THE MODE OF
A PIECE OF POLYPHONY

No theorist has taken the trouble to list the criteria taught during the period for determining the mode of a piece of polyphonic music. Those set out below are the result of an intensive study of Renaissance music.

1. If the work is based on Gregorian themes the mode of these determines the mode of the whole composition.

2. In all other cases the lowest note of the final chord is the surest way of identifying the mode of a piece. If a scale is built up on this note and the key-signature taken into account, in the great majority of cases the mode of the piece will be quite clear. Thus, if the bass concludes on G and there is a flat in the key-signature, it is almost certain that this is the Dorian mode transposed. If the bass finishes on D and there is no flat in the key-signature, the piece is in the natural form of the Dorian mode.

3. The polyphonists rarely use more than one flat in the key-signature. It follows that when there are one or more sharps, or

more than one flat in a polyphonic piece, then quite clearly the piece concerned has been transposed at a later date.

To determine the mode the second rule should be followed. For example, if the piece ends on D and there are two sharps in the key-signature, it belongs to the Lydian mode. (5) If it concludes on C and has two flats as a key-signature it is in the Dorian mode. If it concludes on E with a key-signature of three sharps it belongs to the Mixolydian mode.

4. If the bass descends a minor second at the end of a piece, it is in the Phrygian mode, for example *Missa Quarti toni, Domine non sum dignus*, by Victoria.

5. The third mode very often ends on the chord of its fourth degree—the chord of A replacing the chord of E. Accordingly, the final is in this case the fifth, and not the bass of the concluding chord. The cadence is formed by one of these progressions—I–IV (E–A) or VII–IV (D–A). These may be seen in *Magnificat* by Victoria (*Opera Omnia*, Volume III, Leipzig, 1904, pages 22–31) and *Magnificat* by M. Robledo (S. Rubio, *Antología polifónica sacra*. Madrid, 1956, Vol. II, p. 135).

Note: While few of the Gregorian melodies are written to be sung in a range which would necessitate a key-signature, countless polyphonic works cannot be performed without being transposed to an appropriate pitch. This happens more particularly with the authentic modes.

CHAPTER 7

The *Semitonia*

Having explained concisely the theory of the eight modes in the preceding chapter, as conceived by the writers of mediaeval treatises (from whom those of the sixteenth century received it unaltered), the following chapters deal with a problem closely connected with modality—the *semitonia subintellecta.*

This phrase was used by the theorists of the sixteenth century and earlier when referring to the signs of alteration which—according to contemporary practice—were made by the singers in performance, though they did not appear in the part books.

This practice brought about the collapse of modality and the gradual movement towards modern major–minor tonality.

In the thirteenth century—and even earlier—it became the practice to alter ascending movement by means of the sharp, invented not long before this.

Marchettus of Padua, Nicholas of Capua, Johannes de Muris, Johannes de Garlandia, Prosdocimus de Beldemandis, Giovanni Maria Lanfranco and various others, as well as some anonymous theorists, assert, in one way or another, that all imperfect consonances (thirds and sixths), when followed by perfect consonances (unison, octave, fifth), should be major, in order to achieve smoother progression. This, of course, implies that if the interval in question is minor, it should be altered.

In the fourteenth century the function of the leading note became defined, this giving the ring of an authentic dominant to the chord of which it forms a part.

In this century, and even more so in the next, cadences are found occurring quite naturally on different degrees of the mode. They were used with some caution at first, but later on with real authority and assurance.

At the same time the V–I perfect cadence—more or less

clearly defined—makes its appearance, being in very frequent use by the turn of the sixteenth century.

From the evolutionary process here briefly outlined, it will be clear that the compositions of the Renaissance polyphonists conform only in appearance to the mediaeval theories of the *octoechos*. In practice, although giving them lip service, their procedure was very different from that of the Gregorian modes, in fact it must be acknowledged that they are on the very threshold of modern major–minor tonality.

THE PROBLEM

The *semitonia subintellecta* constitutes one of the most thorny and delicate problems in the transcription of early polyphony.

In spite of the comprehensiveness of the rules given by various authorities they do not cover all cases, and these accordingly are of uncertain solution.

It is not always possible to lay down hard and fast rules about recognized procedures especially after a gap of centuries.

This is so particularly in the case of the Dorian mode, where the sixth is sometimes major, sometimes minor and in many cases doubtful, within the same piece. When composers do not state their intentions clearly there is considerable uncertainty in transcribing cadences formed with a seven-to-six suspension on this same sixth degree.

For these reasons we regard this subject as being worthy of the closest attention.

It is therefore discussed fully and it has been thought advisable to quote, almost in their entirety, the chapters devoted to it by the authors of various treatises.

THE SOURCES

These fall into two categories—theoretical and practical.

The first category comprises musical treatises written by the polyphonists themselves or by contemporary or earlier authors.

In these treatises they define and classify the cadences, they indicate the notes used and show when it is necessary to sharpen some of them because of the nature of the cadence. They study the types of intervals, when (according to the different modes in which they occur) they should be major or minor, and therefore when it is necessary to use the sharp or flat, although it is not expressly shown.

The second category covers the printed polyphony of the late sixteenth and early seventeenth centuries, which is quite explicit in its liberal use of sharps and flats. These printed editions, published during the lifetime and frequently under the supervision of their composers, wholly confirm the theories of the writers of the treatises.

Quotation will be made principally from the treatises of three Spanish authors of the sixteenth century. Because of the early date of the first (more properly regarded as belonging to the fifteenth century), and the authority of the other two, we regard these three as of outstanding importance in the solution of the problems set forth in this chapter. (1)

The first is Francisco Tovar's *Libro de música práctica*, printed in Barcelona in 1510. Chapters VI and VII of this work are of especial interest in connection with the subject we are about to discuss. Even if the wording is at times a trifle obscure, especially because of the absence of examples, once the questions are studied alongside the other authors, Tovar's meaning becomes perfectly clear.

The other two authorities are the Dominican Fr. Tomás de Santa María and the Franciscan Fr. Juan Bermudo.

P. Santa María's work *Arte de tañer fantasia*, though printed in 1565, must be regarded as belonging to the first half of the sixteenth century. It was finished and ready for the printer in 1557, but it was not possible to have it published at that time 'owing to a serious shortage of paper and also for other reasons' ['haber habido gran falta de papel y otras causas']. If the sixteen years it took him to write the book are subtracted from 1557, it must have been started in 1541. This means that the author is describing in his treatise the technique of music before 1550. Apart from being contemporary with our most distinguished composers of polyphony, a point in favour of this work is that it was written and produced with great thoroughness and care. In addition—according to the author—he discussed all his problems with 'men who were skilled and knowledgeable in these matters'.

Here are his words:

In this (referring to the time taken in writing the work) I spent sixteen unbroken years in my prime of life, labouring ceaselessly by day and night, each day reaching conclusions and revising and changing others, so that they should be given perfection of expression in the form of universal rules, discussing things with men skilled and knowledgeable in these matters, especially with your majesty's illustrious musician Antonio de Cabezón, fearing in sincerity and concern lest I be mistaken in some things. (2)

From the titles of this book by P. Santa María and that of Fr. Juan Bermudo—*Declaración de instrumentos musicales*—it might be supposed that these works have nothing to do with vocal polyphony and that the technique shown here applies to instrumental music only. This is not so, as the chapter of Santa María's book in which he explains the cadences is called *De las cláusulas de canto de órgano*, this phrase being used in the sixteenth century to denote what today is called vocal polyphony. Both Santa María and Bermudo devote a chapter to the question of adapting vocal polyphony for performance on the organ, the harp and the *vihuela*; and it is obvious that they would not apply to these works, for instrumental performance, harmonic procedures out of keeping with the attitude and method of working of the composers of polyphony.

In addition, the fact should be borne in mind that the authors wrote their works 'with the intention of mitigating and easing the tremendous difficulty formerly existing, and the great length of time spent in learning to sing and play' [. . . . 'con el fin de remediar y facilitar el gran trabajo que hasta entonces se pasaba y los muchos años que se consumían en saber cantar y tañer']. But there is an even more significant fact. When these authors, especially when they are discussing cadences, quote examples from the music of other composers to confirm their teaching, they choose examples, not from the works of organ composers, but from the vocal works of Gombert, Josquin, Morales, Verdelot, etc.

Bermudo's two books are likewise contemporary with our greatest composers of polyphony, and his *Declaración de instrumentos musicales* claims the distinction, worth bearing in mind, of having been read and approved by Cristóbal de Morales and by Bernardino de Figueroa, *Maestro de Capilla de la Real de Granada*.

The authors in question, despite the fact that they lived and wrote their books in different parts of the country, agreed over instruction concerning the situations where sharps and flats should be used in cadences, and in other passages in their works, whether or not they are expressly indicated. This proves that this view was very commonly held throughout Spain, was acknowledged by all the musicians of the period and, therefore, was followed by composers when writing their music. The same doctrine was recognized and practised in other musical centres in Europe, as can be seen in the case of Italian authorities, to whom the Spaniards refer frequently, and others.

CHAPTER 8

The *Semitonia* in Cadences

THE DEFINITION OF CADENCE
According to Santa María

The important thing is to know whether a cadence comprising three notes, such as DCD, is a concluding or a passing cadence.

There are three important requirements in connection with this cadence. The first is that the first note must be a semibreve and the second a minim, but the third can be any one of the eight note-values.

The second thing is that the semibreve in question should always occur in an upper part and on the concluding beat of the bar. The third is that the minim immediately following the semibreve should move downward by step and then return in the opposite direction, as for example, FEF. It frequently happens that instead of the semibreve in the cadence there is a dotted minim, the descending movement being decorated by a crotchet or two quavers. This ornamentation is added to lend the cadence grace and elegance.

In addition, the cadence is found in two forms, one natural and the other chromatic. The natural cadence is formed with a whole-tone, as in DCD, while the the chromatic form of it was a semitone, as in FEF.

Concerning the chromatic cadence there are two points to be remembered. The first is that it can be formed on any of the five natural notes C, D, F, G, A, but never on E. The other is that the note following the semibreve by downward step must of necessity be a semitone distant from it. This means that in DCD the C, in GFG the F, and in AGA the G must be sharpened.

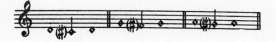

It should also be noted that there are two types of cadence, short and long. The short cadence has been discussed already in its chromatic and natural forms, the long cadence is demonstrated in the following examples. (1)

These are the rules given by Santa María concerning the formation of the melodic part of the cadence. They are so clear and precise that they need no explanation.

Let us now look at the question of when those cadences should use the semitone and when the whole-tone.

Each of the eight modes has its concluding, intermediate and passing cadences. Concluding cadences are those which occur on the final of the mode—intermediate, those on the dominant—and passing cadences are those formed on other notes of the scale.

CADENCES IN EACH MODE

The first mode has its cadences on D, and a fifth higher on A. The cadence on D is a concluding cadence, the one on A intermediate, and both use the semitone.

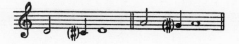

The second mode has its cadences on D, F and A. The cadence on D is a concluding cadence, using the semitone; the cadence on F is intermediate, using the semitone; and the cadence on A is passing, using the whole-tone.

The third mode has its cadences on E, G and C. The cadence on E is a concluding cadence, using the whole-tone; the cadence on G is passing, using the semitone; and the cadence on C is intermediate, using the semitone.

The fourth mode has its cadences on E and a fourth higher on A. The cadence on E is a concluding cadence, using the whole-tone; and the cadence on A is an intermediate cadence, using the semitone.

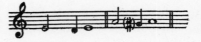

The fifth mode has its cadence on F and a fifth higher on C. The cadence on F is a concluding cadence and that on C intermediate. Both use the semitone.

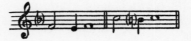

The sixth mode has its cadences on F, on A and on C. The cadence on F is a concluding cadence, using the semitone; the cadence on A is intermediate, using the whole-tone; and the cadence on C is passing, using the semitone.

The seventh mode has its cadences on G and a fifth higher on D. The cadence on G is a concluding cadence and that on D intermediate. Both use the semitone.

The eight mode has its cadences on G and a fourth higher on C. The cadence on G is a concluding cadence and that on C intermediate. Both use the semitone. (2)

Summing up: the concluding cadences—those on the final—in modes I, II, V, VI, VII and VIII use the semitone, and this happens not only at the ends of pieces but whenever any voice has a cadence on the note in question, in any octave.

The intermediate cadences on the notes corresponding to the dominants or reciting tones of modes I, II, III, IV, V, VII and VIII use the semitone. The dominant cadence in mode VI uses the whole-tone (AGA) in order to avoid the interval of diminished third or augmented sixth or, as will be seen later on, because octave or unison should not be approached by simultaneous semitone movement.

The passing cadences on G and C, in modes III and VI respectively, use the semitone, and the cadence on the fifth degree of mode II (E) uses the whole-tone.

And now, what does Tovar have to say?

The first and second modes have cadences on their final, the fifth above it and the octave, and phrases finishing on these notes form appropriate cadences there and nowhere else. And since the first and second modes have D as final, with DCD as the regular cadence in both cases, these notes in such cadences *are separated by a semitone.* Although in the voice part it may appear as a whole-tone, in actual fact it is a semitone. Similarly AGA *will be separated by a semitone.* The third and fourth modes (or tones) form cadences properly on their final which is, of course, E; and because B, the upper limit of its lower fifth, is awkward and frequently harsh in sound as the fourth from F (on account of the tritone formed by the notes F–B) it was agreed to move the cadences which would normally be formed here, higher. A cadence may be formed on A in the fourth mode, as in the first mode;

but the first mode uses the unwritten semitone in this cadence, as has been pointed out above; whereas the fourth mode uses the whole-tone. For this reason the third mode (or tone) uses the cadence on C, and its interval sequence being identical with that of FEF, (3) it already uses a semitone naturally—no accidental is required. Similarly the fifth and sixth modes (or tones), with their finals on F, do not require any understood alteration in any of their cadences, as do the first and second modes (or tones). The seventh and eighth modes have their cadences at the extremities of their scales like all the others previously mentioned and, like the first and second modes, require an accidental in their cadences. Just as the first and second modes use the understood semitone with DCD or AGA, so the seventh and eighth make use of G and D where they form their cadences. In these modes cadences should not be formed on any other note but, as has been pointed out, on the final and fifth above it. This is the case in each mode except the third and fourth, which for the reason given above cadence in different places, as we have said. (4)

It follows from what Tovar says that the semitone is used in concluding cadences in modes I, II, V, VI, VII and VIII, and not in modes III and IV. Santa María and Tovar are in complete agreement on this point. But it may have been possible to observe slight differences between them in respect of intermediate cadences.

According to Tovar the cadence on the fifth degree from the final in mode II is altered, and according to Santa María it is not. The same situation arises with mode IV. These differences are easily explained if it is remembered that some composers write the second mode with a B flat key-signature and others without. If it is written with the flat it is not possible to alter the cadence on A as this would create semitone movement to the unison or octave in two parts. In other words, the invervals of diminished third or augmented sixth, which would arise from the combination of the notes B flat and G sharp, must be avoided. If these modes are written without B flat the cadence will be altered, and the leading note sharpened.

No asÍ:

The other point of difference which may be observed between the two authors is in indicating the position of the intermediate cadences in modes VI and VIII. What Santa María calls passing cadences in modes II, III and IV (which Tovar does not mention at all) are not of any special significance since, as can be seen from the examples given below, and by examination of any polyphonic work one cares to choose, composers frequently formed cadences on notes of the scale other than those indicated by the theorists. (5)

Many composers [says Tovar] all, generally speaking, are more concerned with the sound of the music than with the observance of such rules as these, since it is obvious that in all compositions we find cadences of the first mode in the sixth, and of the fifth mode in the fourth, and so on. We can say, therefore, that there is only one mode (or tone) in singing, since all use the same cadences, as such compositions show. (6)

Santa María says almost the same thing:

Although it is true that all the rules we have given are in fact correct . . ., nevertheless we see that composers sometimes do not observe them. As far as cadences are concerned, those of one mode sometimes become confused with those of another. For example, in the first mode, a fourth mode cadence may be formed on E, as has been done by Verdelot in his motet *Gabriel Archangelus*. Also in the fourth mode a first mode cadence may be formed on D, as Josquin has done in his motet *Miserere mei Deus*, and the same sort of thing happens in all the other modes. Similarly, sometimes the cadences of the authentic modes become confused with those of the plagal modes, and on the other hand plagal modes use authentic cadences. At other times it so happens that composers, looking for something different to do, form cadences which go right outside the mode. As a result there are many works in which the mode is not clear, and accordingly it is impossible to determine which mode they are in. Examples of this can be seen in *Si bona suscepimus* by Verdelot, and in many other works. (7)

From the foregoing it may be deduced:

1. that there are whole-tone or unaltered cadences and semitone or sharpened cadences;
2. that concluding cadences in modes having as their tonic or final notes D, F and G, or their transposed equivalents, always use the semitone;

E

3. *that the penultimate note in these cadences must be transcribed with a sharp (or equivalent sign if the piece has been transposed),* even if this is not found written in the manuscripts or printed editions, *this being understood;*

4. that concluding cadences in modes having their final on E are unaltered;

5. that besides these cadences on the final notes of the modes, there are others called intermediate or passing cadences, for which the writers of treatises give set notes in each mode corresponding to the dominants or reciting tones in the Gregorian modes, and that these all use the semitone except that of mode VI which retains the whole-tone; and

6. that composers, according to the testimony of those same authorities, frequently form cadences on notes of the mode other than those indicated, and moreover that they confuse those of one mode with another.

The polyphonic composers use cadences mainly at the ends of sentences, phrases and more important sections of a work, placing these as a general rule at those points where the text gives, to a greater or lesser degree, a sense of finality.

According to Santa María, there is yet another passing cadence which can be formed:

> . . . on any degree of the scale in each mode, subject to two conditions. One is that the highest and lowest voices should never conclude the cadence at the octave or double octave, but only at the tenth. But any one of the other intermediate voices may well conclude the cadence at the octave below the highest part. This applies when the passing cadence is formed outside the mode, because when it is formed within the mode bass and soprano can quite satisfactorily conclude with a perfect concord, i.e. either octave or twelfth, or one of their compounds. The other condition is that after the cadence has occurred the music should move on immediately, so that it is only passing, and thus such a cadence as this is really progression rather than cadence. (8)

The most frequent of these is what we would call today the resolution of a chord having the function of a dominant resolving by step upwards.

The following problem now arises: accepting the fact that composers in their works frequently formed intermediate cadences on notes other than those indicated by the theorists, and, that in Santa María's opinion passing cadences can be formed on any degree of the scale, how is it possible to distinguish altered from unaltered cadences and thence to know when it is necessary to add the sharp in transcription and when it is not?

The authors quoted do not lay down a firm rule covering each and every case. They examined the cadences for the number of dissonances present in their accompanying harmony, these indicating, in each case, whether the cadence is formed by whole-tone or semitone movement.

So, from the different cases they study and the examples they use to illustrate their teachings, it is possible to work out rules for distinguishing between cadences. These rules cover all cadences—concluding, intermediate and passing cadences in all modes—and are based on the harmony with which the polyphonists accompany the melodic part of the cadence.

Considered from this point of view the cadences are treated almost always in these ways:

1. As a four-to-three suspension within a major triad in 5/3 position, whose bass moves by the intervals of rising fourth or descending fifth. In this formula the cadence invariably uses the semitone no matter on what note it is formed.

2. The bass of this chord may ascend by step. This produces the real passing (= interrupted) cadence, which also always uses the semitone.

3. As a seven-to-six suspension within a six–three chord when the bass moves downward by step. This cadence may be either altered or unaltered. It is sharpened if the bass descends a major second, unaltered if the movement in the bass is a minor second. (9)

When the cadence is found in the bass, if the interval which makes the suspension with the third of the six–three chord which follows is a major second, its cadence is sharpened, otherwise it is unaltered.

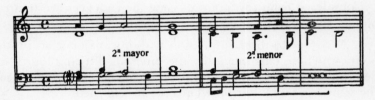

If the cadence makes a nine-to-eight suspension it is always unaltered.

The most commonly used cadences are the first three shown. Of the first of these Santa María says: 'that it is the most used and the most frequently found in all music'. (10)

The rules for dealing with those cases in which the cadence does not actually form a suspension, but where each of the notes is accompanied by a different consonant chord, will be considered in the following chapter.

THE USE OF CADENCES

Cadences are used very frequently by the composers of polyphony—even the shortest composition has its share of them. Examination of the shortest motet or responsory of Victoria or any other composer will reveal six, seven or even more. The writers of treatises recommend their frequent use for the smoothness they lend the music.

> All song [says Bermudo] should be graced with many cadences, and sometimes they assist its smooth flow. The song is harmonious in proportion to the number of cadences it contains. The cadences are so strong by reason of their perfection that they make dissonance sound consonant. (11)

THE *SEMITONIA* IN THE CONCLUDING BAR

All that has been said up to this point refers to the penultimate bar in cadences.

But what of their concluding chords? Are they major or minor? Concluding chords of intermediate or passing cadences will not be dealt with here, because in fully understanding them other rules must be taken into account. These will be considered in the next chapter.

It should, however, be made quite clear that the final chord of a polyphonic work of the sixteenth century must always be major. Thus do P. Santa María and Fr. Juan Bermudo affirm it categorically:

> Compositions generally conclude with an octave (the melodic distance between bass and soprano) or with a double octave, *the harmonization of which must be major. To this end, one of the middle voices, either tenor or contralto, must sing the major third.* This makes the harmony sound strong and clear. (12)

And this is how Fr. Juan Bermudo puts it:

> Then we may say . . . that just as we may begin with imperfect consonances, (13) so we may conclude with them, especially *the major third, which is so perfectly suited for this use that there is hardly* a four-part cadence in which one voice does not remain on the major tenth. (14)

CHAPTER 9

Use of the *Semitonía* apart
from Cadences

It is not only in cadences that the polyphonists make use of the implied or understood semitone. There are, in their works, many other passages implying the presence of a sharp or flat, though these are not actually written in front of the notes requiring them.

All the authors consulted agree about the laws set out below; only in one case is there a slight difference of opinion between Spanish and non-Spanish scholars.

Because of this agreement among authorities and also for the sake of brevity, the only transcription given will be of Chap. 38 of Fr. Juan Bermudo's work *Arte tripharia* (Osuna, 1550). (1)

It should be pointed out, nevertheless, that Tovar's testimony, which for the reasons given above will not be transcribed, is doubly important, inasmuch as this author, in Chap. 6 of his work, asserts that the laws governing and regulating the intervals in their progression have been 'established by our illustrious predecessors' ['determinación de nuestros claros predecesores'], and that they were applied similarly in Saragossa, Sicily and Rome 'by many outstanding men, competent in this sphere' ['con muchos especiales hombres y aptos en esta facultad'].

From this we gather that they were recognized throughout Europe in the fifteenth and sixteenth centuries. (2)

The occasions, apart from cadences, where, according to the treatise writers, each note should bear a sharp or flat, although these signs are not actually written in polyphonic printed music and manuscripts, are as follows:

1. When a harmonic interval of the third (C–E) resolves by conjunct and contrary motion onto a unison (D), the third in

question should be minor, provided always that no other voice makes this impossible. (3)

This is usually achieved, according to the theorists, by raising the lower voice a semitone. The same thing applies if voices a tenth apart move simultaneously onto an octave.

2. If a third (D–F) proceeds, by contrary and conjunct movement to a fifth (C–G), the third should be major. (4)

3. Likewise, if a third (D–F) is followed by an octave with one of the voices moving by leap of a fifth and the other by step, the third in question will also be major.

4. Whenever a fifth (D–A) is followed by a sixth (D–B) returning to the same fifth, the interval of the sixth should be minor. The higher middle note is lowered by means of a flat or natural in those cases where the movement is made by the upper voice. If the movement is made by the lower voice the effect is achieved by raising the middle note by means of a sharp or natural.

5. Every sixth moving by conjunct contrary motion to an octave will be major. (5)

These are the most common and most important rules governing the progression of these intervals. They are all based on what the theorists call the law of the closest proximity in the voice-parts or, to put it differently, any perfect consonance (unison, fifth or octave) should be preceded by the imperfect consonance nearest to it. (6) Thus the octave G–G will not be preceded by the minor sixth A–F, but by the major sixth A–F sharp, which is closer to it than the minor sixth.

Chapter 38 of Fr. Juan Bermudo's *Arte tripharia*, in which he sets out the rules listed above, now follows. These are his words:

Whenever I have cause to write the unison or one of its compounds following a third or one of its compounds, I do not use the major third, which is perfect, but the minor third, which is called imperfect. The minor third is nearer to the unison than the major third. Therefore, if in the music we find a major third moving to a unison, this [interval] should neither be played nor sung. Generally, when we find this major third which must be made minor, this is done in the lower part by playing the note concerned on the black key above it. This same procedure is followed in moving to an octave from a tenth, and to a fifteenth from a seventeenth. If I find it necessary to write a fifth, approaching it from a third, the third will be major, that is to say perfect, this major third being nearer to the fifth than the minor third.

If in printed music we find the above-mentioned major third (say F–A, moving to E–B) it will remain as it has been written. If the third is minor, adjustment will be made in the upper voice, raising this to the black key nearest to the written note. If there is any obstacle to the performance of this note in any octave, adjustment will be made in the lower voice, with the black key that lowers it a semitone. (7) Generally this rule of the major third will be maintained when we move from a third to an octave.

If from a fifth we move to a sixth and then return to the fifth again, we make the sixth minor (that is, imperfect) because this is nearer to the fifth. If the upper voice makes the movement to the sixth and this is not a minor sixth in the printed music, it should be made so with a black key which lowers it a semitone. If the lower voice makes the movement to a sixth which is not a minor sixth, it should be made so by use of a black key which raises it a semitone. If the lower voice moves to a sixth and we have the minor sixth on the white keys, this is how it will be performed, but if not it must be played with a black key, that is, the sharp nearest to the white note.

Whenever we write an octave (either in the cadence, or in passing) moving from the sixth, we shall use a major sixth (that is to say, perfect) which is nearer to the octave than the minor sixth.

If it is written this way no difficulty arises. If it is not in the written music, adjustment must be made in the upper voice with a black key sharpening it. If for some particular reason it is not possible to make such an adjustment, this must be made in the lower voice with a black key, flattening it. In this case a fourth mode cadence will be formed, concluding in the lower voice with a semitone and in the upper voice with a whole-tone. . . .

The procedure I have followed in simple intervals should be followed also in compound intervals. The unison is approached from the minor third, the octave from the minor tenth, and similarly with all compound intervals. As the octave is the compound of the unison so the twelfth is of the fifth.

The above-mentioned rule should be observed strictly, unless this creates dissonance where there should be perfect consonance. I call fifth, octave and all their compounds perfect consonances. In these cases the above-mentioned rule is not observed, and notes will be performed as printed. An example showing both rule and exception is given. (8)

One difference of opinion, to which we referred earlier, is found between Spanish authors and a non-Spaniard. This concerns the third moving by contrary motion to the fifth. According to Spanish authors the interval in question must be major, by reason of its closer proximity to the fifth, while Zarlino would have it minor, to avoid the tritone arising from it. (9) What then should be the procedure in transcription?

It is by no means an easy problem to solve since each composer would follow the laws with which he was familiar. But surely it is not likely that Zarlino's theory would be unknown to Spanish writers and composers, in view of the number of Spanish musicians who visited Italy.

On the other hand, in Tovar the rule to which we refer is set forth as clearly as in Bermudo, and we certainly know that the latter spent some time in Sicily and Rome, discussing it with musicians in those places.

And this is not all. In the printed works of Palestrina, Victoria, Lassus and others the major third, expressly indicated, leading to the fifth, can often be seen. In Palestrina's famous *Stabat Mater* for eight voices there are many examples. In the work of Victoria they are encountered at every turn, and it would be very easy to quote innumerable passages from other composers.

Having examined the rules ordering the succession of intervals, we can easily solve two cases, the solution of which was deferred when studying cadences.

First, there is the question of knowing whether a cadence is altered or unaltered, when the second half of the first of the three notes forming the cadence in question does not actually form a suspension, but is accompanied by a separate chord, different from those which precede and follow it, or when one voice has the melodic outline DCD, GFG or AGA, without satisfying the required conditions for being able to regard it as an authentic cadence in the sense in which this is defined by Santa María. (10)

It is obvious then that the note which needs to be altered is always the third of a triad in five-three position, whose bass moves by the intervals of descending fifth or ascending fourth, or the sixth of a six-three chord whose bass descends by step.

In the first two cases the cadence is invariably sharpened by virtue of the third rule given above.

If, on occasion, the chord in question is followed by another in five-three position, with the bass descending, this cadence is also sharpened, providing that the note to be altered makes a third with the bass and proceeds to a fifth by contrary motion. It follows, by virtue of the second rule studied in this chapter, that this third should be major, this being closer to the fifth than the minor third.

When the note to be altered is the sixth of a six-three chord, the cadence will be sharpened or unaltered according to whether the bass descends a major or a minor second.

The second question awaiting solution is the nature of the final chord in intermediate cadences. It should be possible to determine whether this particular chord should be major, as in final cadences, or whether it should be minor.

In deciding this the chord immediately following it must be kept in mind. If it is followed by another chord in five-three position, with falling fifth or rising fourth progression between the bass notes of the two chords, the final chord of an intermediate cadence will be major, always assuming that it contains an interval of the third between the bass and one of the upper voices. This interval, then, must be major, by virtue of the third rule given above.

This explains the successions of three, four and more major chords in five-three position with fourth or fifth progression between their bass notes, found in the music of the polyphonists. In each of the chords in the series there is always a third between the lowest and one of the upper voices. This third must without fail be major, so that it can be followed in the same voices by an octave.

The final chord in intermediate cadences is also major if it is followed by another in five-three position, with descending contrary motion in the bass. As in the former instance this contains a third between the bass and one of the upper voices. This is followed by a fifth and it is quite obvious why the first should be major.

* * * * *

In making transcriptions according to the rules given up to this point some difficulties can arise, such as the following:

1. Inexact correspondence of the intervals in imitation.

2. The chromaticism arising out of the application of the rules given above.

As far as the first is concerned it sometimes happens that not only do the intervals of a theme and its answer not correspond, but that repetition of the same motif does not result in exact repetition of the size of the intervals, this being prevented by another voice transcribed with the accidentals required by the theme, or because the theme by itself cannot carry the accidentals required by the imitation.

Motete "Doctor bonus" Victoria.

From this a doubt may arise concerning the application of the rules studied above, since if a theme is repeated without being identical with its first statement though using the same notes, it appears to argue against their authority.

Nevertheless we cannot allow that this objection has any real force. To support our arguments we have printed music of the latter part of the sixteenth century, in which the accidentals in a theme are expressly shown, but are not reproduced in its imitations, their use being prevented by another voice or other voices.

The following works of Victoria may be examined, *O quam gloriosum est regnum* for four voices, bars 46 et seq.; *O magnum mysterium* for four voices, from bar 28 to the end; *Missa Quarti toni* for four voices, bar 11 of Hosanna. In the 1572 edition of the motets quoted, and in the 1592 edition of *Missa Quarti toni*, the accidentals in the theme are expressly indicated, but cannot be reproduced in the answer because of another voice. Others are given in the imitation but do not appear in the theme itself.

CHAPTER 10

Chromatic Progression

In the previous chapter we have shown that the fact that the theme and its imitations do not correspond is no obstacle to the application of the rules concerning the understood or implied semitone.

But what if in some situation the application of those principles should give rise to chromatic progression? Will the transcriptions made in accordance with them be in keeping with the character of Renaissance polyphony?

It has been customary among scholars not to admit to those procedures in the works of sixteenth-century composers. This attitude is due to studying the polyphonic works as they appear in the transcription of manuscripts and early printed editions— containing very few accidentals—without any sort of reference to the evidence of the theoretical works, many of which were unknown until quite recently. We cannot subscribe to these theories—still less to the idea that the composers were not familiar with the works of contemporary theorists. It is quite certain that they did know them, that in some cases the composers themselves wrote those treatises and that in many cases they approved the works in question, whose use as manuals of instruction they praised unreservedly. On the other hand if it is certain that the diatonicism of Gregorian chant had, at first, an influence on the modal conceptions of *Ars nova*, it is no less certain that in the sixteenth century just the opposite happened. The new conquests of polyphony in the modal sphere were applied to Gregorian chant, at that time in an advanced state of decadence. These included, for example, the raising by a semitone of the seventh degree of the scale in modes I, II, VII and VIII, and even chromatic progression. Various examples could be quoted in support of this statement, but will be omitted for reasons of space, quite apart from the fact that this is so well known to Gregorian scholars that proof is unnecessary.

For these reasons, and especially because of the evidence of the great theorist Fr. Juan Bermudo, quoted below, we regard the opinion of those who completely exclude chromatic progression from the works of the polyphonists as being entirely without foundation, especially as far as those of the second half of the sixteenth century are concerned. On the contrary, the printed editions and even some manuscripts of this period, quite explicit in their use of sharps and flats, support the view given earlier.

ASCENDING CHROMATIC PROGRESSION

In Chap. 32 of his *Declaración de instrumentos musicales*, Bermudo deals with the use of dissonances, among which he includes a chromatic ascending interval of the second, a 'major semitone', whose use he justifies by the application of the rules governing interval succession explained in the preceding pages. Here are Bermudo's words:

I find three kinds of seconds in the composition of polyphony, and each in its place is satisfactory. . . . The third type of second is the major semitone. This method of using it (not harmonically, but in the melodic progression of a single voice, as it is used in the chromatic style) has come back into favour again. In Spain it has not been used—I have not actually seen it written—although it has certainly been used, as I said, in the chromatic style. (1) Where it is properly prepared we can use this major semitone as shown in the following example:

Whoever studies the above example closely will find that this so-called unsingable semitone occurs three times. To make it clear how this semitone is prepared, and how it can be used whenever we wish to do so, three points should be noted. The first is that it should not be called the unsingable semitone as this implies that it is literally impossible to sing, but should be described as being out-of-keeping with the diatonic style. But, as what is played and sung nowadays may be a mixture of diatonic and chromatic styles, there is room for such a semitone. Secondly, I assume that in progression to an octave from a sixth, the sixth will be major, and not minor, provided there is no impediment to this. The third point is that the augmented fifth should not be used in music which makes any claim to be well written. Once these three points are accepted, the example is quite clear. The minim (crotchet) C in the tenor part should be sharpened, but because the bassus has another minim (crotchet) on F at the distance of a fifth it is not possible to sharpen the C as this would create an augmented fifth. The third minim (crotchet) in the tenor, on D, makes an octave with the semibreve (minim) of the bass on D, and it is preceded by the sixth, E–C, which should be major. It follows that the second minim (crotchet) C in the tenor part must be played with a black key. Thus, by means of placing the first minim on white and the second on a black key, the major semitone is played. Also, by this device the second minim (crotchet) of the altus, F sharp, and the second minim (crotchet) of the cantus, C (sharp), are played, and even sung by some, without realizing it. Thus, although both notes are printed with the same sign (for different reasons), one is played with a white key and the other with a black.

The above-mentioned procedures will not in any way disturb those who understand chromatic music. (2)

It will be seen that the chromatic progression of the example given and explained by Bermudo arises out of the rules given in the previous chapter.

In addition, the following works, published in *Suplimento Polifónico*, should be examined: Number 1, *Quam pulchri sunt*, for six voices, by A. Lobo, bar 26; number 3, *Tantum ergo*, for four equal voices, by P. M. Cardoso, bar 23; *Et incarnatus est*, by the same composer, bar 12; number 10, *Christus factus est*, for four equal voices, Palestrina (?), bar 39.

In all these examples the ascending chromatic progression

occurs—most frequently—when the bass proceeds in one of the following ways:

(*a*) From a five–three chord: descent of a minor third followed by rising movement of perfect fourth or second, being in each case the bass of a five–three chord.

Misa,"Vidi speciosam" Victoria.

(*b*) Ascending movement of a major third followed by another—also ascending—of perfect fourth or descending fifth, these being as in the previous case, five–three chords.

Motete "Sancta Maria", Victoria.

The first of these contrapuntal procedures is the more common. There is another succession of chromatic steps brought about by different contrapuntal procedures that are not easy to group under a common formula.

Having examined the examples given it can be deduced that, apart from two or three, all the instances of chromaticism so far encountered among the hundreds of works consulted from the different polyphonic schools of the sixteenth century arise exclusively from application of the rules governing interval succession, already well known. Therefore, on the basis of Bermudo's authority and the clear examples found in printed editions and manuscripts, we consider that those laws can be

F

applied with reasonable assurance of accuracy in transcribing polyphonic music, even if, occasionally, these give rise to passing chromatic movement not expressly indicated in the original copies.

DESCENDING CHROMATIC PROGRESSION

Descending chromatic progression also occurs fairly frequently, although we have not seen any reference to this in the works of the theorists. But the printed editions and manuscripts of the second half of the sixteenth century provide us with examples. The most common is found in fourth mode cadences whose concluding chord is always major. It sometimes happens that the note affected by a sharp reappears in the following chord, in the same part—not as the third but as the fifth or a doubling of the bass, making in each case the descent of a minor second, and creating a chromatic step.

It can also occasionally happen that when a chord is repeated the voice having the third begins a descending outline of certain notes, this giving rise as in the previous instance, to a chromatic interval. The object of this is to avoid an augmented second, as may be seen in the following example:

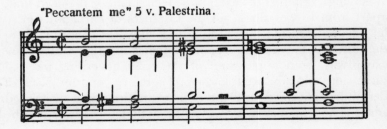

AUGMENTED AND DIMINISHED INTERVALS

The strict use of the *semitonía* (i.e. the implied or under-stood semitone) can give rise to intervals of augmented fourth and of diminished fourth and fifth, a situation that did not pass unnoticed by the theorists. Hence the fact that Bermudo devotes a chapter of his *Declaración de instrumentos musicales* to explaining and justifying its legitimate use.

The interval of the diminished fourth is the one that can occur most frequently, and this happens especially in resolving the altered note in cadences. For example, instead of DCD the cadence can move DCF, this resulting in an interval of the diminished fourth between the notes C and F when the C is sharpened, as is normal procedure in cadences.

Some performers use this same interval of a tone and two minor semitones (i.e. the diminished fourth) by leap in one voice only (though in fear and trembling), because it appears to them to be contrary to accepted procedure to use the leap of a fourth other than that of two and a half tones (i.e. the perfect fourth). In order both to reassure them and instruct beginners I say it is possible to use it, and if it is inappropriate in diatonic music it is not contrary to the nature of semi-chromatic music, which is what concerns us most these days. And in order to understand it more clearly they should study the following example:

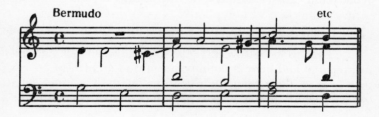

Altus and cantus have this type of fourth (i.e. diminished), and this happened because the cadence with the bassus begun by the altus was completed by the tenor, and the cadence with the tenor begun by the cantus was completed by the altus. There is no interval used more than this fourth when the line moves by step, and it happens whenever we sharpen the lower note in a fourth.... As it is used so much in step-wise movement I do not see why it should not be used by leap, especially when it is associated with an interrupted cadence, as in the above example. I give as a definite rule, that in polyphony a part can use this progression, conceived in terms of stepwise movement (especially on the organ, where it can certainly be done) as a direct leap, when it is properly prepared. (3)

As well as in the preceding example this interval can occur in the course of the following progressions: chords V–I, I–IV and V–III in the Dorian mode and in I–IV and I–VI in the Phrygian mode.

All these progressions are used by Victoria fairly frequently and always, or in most cases, with explicit indication of the interval of the diminished fourth.

As to the intervals of augmented fourth and diminished fifth, which Bermudo also explains and defends, we have not so far encountered any examples in the works of the sixteenth-century composers of polyphony.

Nevertheless Bermudo asserts concerning them:

. . . Hold as incontrovertible the rule that when such movement is prepared and there is no impediment to it, all [these intervals] can be used, these being quite consistent with the semi-chromatic style in which nowadays we play and sing in composition. (4)

CHAPTER II

The Underlaying of Text

THE PROBLEM

The underlaying of text is a most difficult problem especially when transcriptions are based on manuscripts or printed editions earlier than about 1540.

The printed editions of the second half of the sixteenth century, with few exceptions, do not present any major difficulties, since the text in these is fitted to the music just as carefully as at the present day.

This is not so with manuscripts, which are at times so haphazard in matching words and music that a phrase of seven, eight or more syllables will be found under four or five notes, this being followed by a long passage of music with no text at all.

In other cases, a certain phrase of text repeated two or three times with the same melodic phrase is set to it differently in each repetition.

When text is repeated, unless the musical phrase is particularly clear, it is often difficult to decide where a phrase ends and where the next repetition or the following phrase begins.

Of course, this is not absolutely vital in the interpretation of polyphony provided that there is only one singer to each part, for then, although the text may not be correctly matched with the music, at least there will be no disagreement. (1) But what if, instead of only one singer, there are several voices on each part? How can the unanimity in diction essential for the artistic performance of a vocal work be achieved if the books from which it is sung do not provide an answer to this problem?

These brief reflections are, in themselves, enough to prove what we already know from historical documents: that composers and singers had definite and precise procedures for the underlaying of words to music. These were passed on from teacher to pupil and were known almost throughout Europe by the end of the fifteenth and the beginning of the sixteenth century. (2)

These procedures, accepted by all schools, were later collated in their treatises by some theorists, thanks to whom they are available today.

THE SOURCES OF INFORMATION

In the case of what is called the *understood* or *implied semitone* and *chromatic progression*, the Spanish writers are invaluable, dealing as they do with these matters in clear and positive terms. However, in connection with the matter now in hand it is necessary to turn to others, especially the Italians, as among Spanish scholars there is not a single one who codified or handed on tradition in this matter, so important to a proper interpretation of polyphony. (3)

It is quite certain that Spanish composers, singers and theorists were not unaware of the procedures currently in use in this connection among the musicians of the various European schools; and this conviction is based on the frequent intercourse between Spanish polyphonists and those of other nations. This took place, on the one hand, with the Italians, within whose chapels Spanish singers and composers were frequently found, and on the other hand with the Netherlands musicians who came to Spain in great numbers at the beginning of the reign of Philip the Fair. Their compositions were sung in chapels throughout the country, as can be gathered from the great number of those preserved in the archives of Spanish cathedrals and convents.

Also, it is quite possible, in fact certain, that the Spanish schools of music had their own particular tradition and procedure in this connection, as they had in others, these being what might be called the 'mysteries of the guild'. However, as these are unknown today, it is reasonable to base a summary of procedure on those generally practised.

Three Italian theorists—Zarlino, Vicentino and Steffano Vanneo—hand on to posterity the traditional rules.(4) Together with Zacconi these are the most important Italian writers on music in the Renaissance.

However, for reasons of brevity, and especially because Zarlino sums up the traditional ideas concisely in ten rules, discussion will centre chiefly on him. Some details, nevertheless, are included from the work of Vicentino with examples given in his treatise.

THE TEN RULES OF ZARLINO (5)

1. Always place the long or short syllable below an appropriate note, so that no crudeness may be in evidence, since in polyphony any singable note (6) that is not tied, but on its own, except for the crotchet and all notes of lesser value, may carry its own syllable.

This means, of course, that long syllables should fall on notes of longer duration than short syllables. The former can be paired with semibreves and the latter with minims, or the former with minims and the latter with crotchets.

Vanneo's recommendation is similar:

It should also be noted by the best composer(s) that he (they) should arrange that the long syllable of the setting go with the semibreve and the short syllable with the minim, or that the minim is used with the long one and the crotchet with the short, so that the pairing of notes with words avoids any crudeness of procedure. For some composers are often in the habit of putting, most ineptly, short syllables with semibreves and long ones with minims, in their songs. . . . (7)

2. In each ligature of more than one note only one syllable should be given to it, at the beginning.

3. No syllable should be given to the dot which alters notes in counterpoint, although as far as duration is concerned it may be singable, the reason being that it is part of the note affected by it.

4. Rarely does one sing a new syllable to a crotchet, to notes of lesser value or to the note immediately following them.

This rule consists of two points, the first being that it is not usual to pair a new syllable with a crotchet nor with any note of lesser value, the second that rarely is a separate syllable allotted to the note following a crotchet although this may be of greater value.

The study of this rule in the light shed on it by the musical editions of the second half of the sixteenth century make it possible to establish that certain exceptions were allowed.

(*a*) In words in which the accent falls on the antepenultimate syllable, the syllable following the accent is sung to a crotchet, sometimes on a repetition of a previous note, sometimes in motifs of differing melodic construction.

Do - mi- nus. Psal - li- te no - mi- ni. Ce - ci- dit.

Su - spen- di- mus or - ga- na. Sta - bu- lo pro-ponitur.

Innumerable examples of this sort can be quoted.

(*b*) Then, in normally accented words (i.e. words whose accent falls on the penultimate syllable), and in combinations of these with those in which the accent falls on the antepenultimate syllable, and of both of these with monosyllables, a syllable may be sung to a crotchet.

Cu - i ta- li- a. Com - me - mo-ra- tionem. In præ-se- pi- o.

Et in cæ- lis In - ve- ni - sti. Qui tol - lis pec-ca - ta.

In all these cases it is quite proper to assign another syllable to the note following the crotchet, so that there is no awkwardness of rhythm. The sixth rule of Zarlino permits this.

(*c*) Quite frequently a new syllable goes with the first notes of a group of crotchets two or more in number.

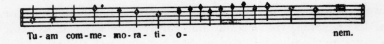

Tu - am com-me- mo-ra- ti- o-   nem.

(*d*) Both long and short groups of crotchets can be found, used for descriptive purposes, each crotchet having a separate syllable. Typical examples are found in those works called 'misas de batalla' or works of this sort. Victoria's *Missa Pro victoria* for nine voices is a case in point.

In addition to the examples given below reference should

be made to the motet *Ardens est cor meum* and the responsory *Una hora*, by Victoria, in which illustrative ideas abound.

(*e*) In sacred settings of the vernacular, such as *villancicos*, *canciones*, *villanescas* and others the practice of giving a separate syllable to each crotchet is common. (See our *Canciones espirituales*, Vols. I and II, Madrid, 1955–6.)

The second part of rule four of Zarlino is given again—'seldom is a separate syllable allotted to the note following a crotchet although this may be of greater value'.

Vicentino gives this rule also in his treatise. (8)

Very occasionally exceptions to this procedure are found in some composers, for example Lassus, Palestrina, Victoria, Guerrero, Castro, Goudimel, etc., the issue here being use of the single crotchet or of groups of two or more. In each case these are followed by notes of longer duration. Consequently the new syllable should not fall on the first of these notes but on the second or third:

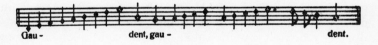

By way of complementing this rule, certain outlines are written in different rhythmic patterns depending on whether the word concerned is accented normally or has the accent on the antepenultimate syllable:

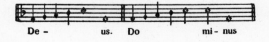

5. One does not allot a syllable to notes lesser in value than the dots which go with a semibreve or minim, such as the crotchet

after the dot of the semibreve and the quaver after the dot of the minim, nor to those following immediately after such notes:

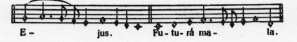

6. When it is necessary to allot a syllable to a crotchet, another can be given to the following note.

7. Any note placed at the beginning of a piece, or after a rest during the course of it, must be accompanied by articulation of a new syllable.

8. In polyphony repetitions are allowed; not of single syllables or words, but of any part of the text whose sense is complete, and this may occur when there are sufficient notes for it to happen comfortably, although repetition is something which (to my way of thinking) is not especially effective, unless it is done, principally, to emphasize words containing an important idea.

This has been noted already in discussion of rule four.

Vicentino also expressed his disapproval of unnecessary repetitions—those not required by the necessity for giving emphasis to a word or phrase. (9)

As a general rule, no repetitions should be introduced other than those expressly indicated in the sources by the signs discussed earlier.

9. When all the syllables in a clause or one part of the text have been satisfactorily allotted to the singable notes, and only the penultimate and final syllables are left, the penultimate syllable may be given to a group of smaller notes, for example, two, three or more, on condition that the syllable in question is long and not short, for if it is short this will be a crude procedure and allotting these notes in this way would constitute an infraction of our first rule.

The first rule says that each note should carry its own syllable. Here, on the contrary, one syllable is permitted to support a melisma, providing the syllable concerned is long. For long syllables are accented, as can be seen from the printed editions.

10. The final syllable of the text should, in accordance with the procedures listed above, coincide with the concluding note of the melody.

There are many cases where the final syllable does not co-incide with the final note.

This always occurs when, at the conclusion of a phrase there remains for the final syllable only a group of crotchets followed by a long note. In this case the final syllable does not fall on the long note (which would be an infringement of the second part of rule four), but on the first of the crochets:

Sometimes phrases conclude with a group of three notes, the first being a dotted minim, the second a crotchet and the third, one of the longer notes. In this case the text may be accommodated as shown in the printed editions:

It is not appropriate to allot syllables of the same word to two notes forming a wide interval, such as a fifth or sixth, and this must always be guarded against if possible with the interval of the octave. Accordingly the word should be concluded on the first note of the interval, so that the following word may begin on the second note.

Vicentino supports this contention. (10)

We point out nevertheless that some polyphonists, scrupulous in their observance of the other rules, disregard this advice of Vicentino, as may be seen in the following passage from Guerrero:

It is clear that in this and other similar examples the application of rule four justifies this infringement.

Where notes are repeated several times at the same pitch, a new syllable goes with each repetition, and if there are only two notes a separate syllable should at least be given to the second.

It must be pointed out, however, that in certain melodic shapes repeated notes are sung to the same syllable. These notes were described technically by the theorists of the fifteenth and preceding centuries as 'repercussae', the term deriving possibly from the reiteration of the distrophes, tristrophes and other groups of notes at the same pitch practised in Gregorian chant.

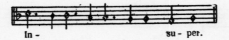

To find out on which note the repetition of a word or different words or even of a complete phrase should begin when this is indicated in the manuscripts and printed editions with the generally accepted signs, one must pay special attention to the musical phrasing, the imitations between the different voices, the intervals, the closes or cadences, the accentuation of the words, etc.

All these details must be taken into account, to solve the problems presented by polyphonic manuscripts in connection with the underlaying of text. And it must not be forgotten that the polyphonists left the singers a certain amount of freedom, so that they could display their vocal powers in the performance of the polyphonic compositions.

Here is given, as an illustration of what has been said, the example cited by Vicentino in this connection in his work from which we have quoted previously.

Part II

Musical Forms of Classical Polyphony

CHAPTER 12

The General Theory
of Musical Forms

The study of the musical forms of polyphony comprises two main parts, the first dealing with the general theory of musical forms, and the second with particular or applied theory concerning them. They will be dealt with separately. The general theory of musical forms is divided into two parts—the materials of construction, common, generally speaking, to all forms, and the organization of the polyphonic fabric as a whole.

THE MATERIALS OF CONSTRUCTION

Everything used by the composer in the erection of his structure is listed under materials of construction. The most important of these are *modality, harmony, counterpoint, themes, text* and *rhythm*.

MODALITY AND TONALITY

This topic has already been discussed. But it must be enlarged upon, so that some aspects of it which did not come within the scope of Chap. 6 may be dealt with adequately.

Polyphonic music is based—more in appearance than in actuality—on the modal scales.

Modality passed through a serious crisis during the sixteenth century or, to put it more accurately, this crisis, which had begun much earlier, became much more acute during the golden age of polyphony.

In their works the polyphonists introduce frequent chromaticisms quite foreign to the natural character of the modal scales, both when the themes are freely composed and when they are taken from Gregorian or popular sources.

Missa Quarti toni of Victoria, a work based on original themes, is quite widely known. Although this is written in the Hypo-phrygian mode—b, c, d, E, f, g, a, b,—G sharp, an element foreign to the scale of the fourth mode, is nevertheless heard constantly throughout its length. And this is not the only note to be altered. Even a cursory glance will reveal various others—F sharp, C sharp and B flat.

But if the works based on Gregorian melodies are examined the result is even more significant. The leading note—the seventh degree in the authentic modes and the third degree in the plagal modes—is regularly raised a semitone, acting as a genuine leading note, this having been regarded as necessary since the fourteenth century.

There is still another factor which contributes powerfully to the breaking down of modal propriety and procedure; namely, modulation or the forming of cadences. Some cadences had become so generally accepted that it is rare to find a piece in which they do not sometimes occur. These include, harmonic-ally speaking, those on the dominant and subdominant.

In any case, with any one of the eight modes, modulations to related modes (i.e. cadences proper to other modes) are frequent.

Other elements destructive of modality are false relations and chromatic intervals, the former being more frequent than the latter.

A natural by-product of the disappearance of modal characteristics is the emergence of functional harmony.

The chord including the leading-note acquires a very con-siderable importance—its rôle as the dominant is confirmed.

At the beginning of the second half of the sixteenth century the polyphonists—to a greater or lesser degree conscious of the significance of what they were doing—used a number of harmonic procedures which anticipate the tonal system: the perfect cadence is in current use; at times it is followed by the plagal cadence; the dominant chord is frequently preceded by the subdominant; a six–three, sometimes a six–five chord is formed on the subdominant (fourth degree) preceding the six–four on the dominant; harmonic progressions, as such, are beginning to be used.

It is quite clear that a good deal of ground must yet be covered before arriving at a positive plan based on the play of tonal functions, but the first steps have been taken with confidence.

HARMONY

The harmonic vocabulary of the sixteenth century was not extensive.

Only one chord was recognized as such—the major or minor triad and its two inversions; the first—the six–three chord—in most common use; the second—the six–four chord—commonly, but not exclusively, used in cadences, with the fourth always prepared.

The diminished triad occurs as the result of a suspension in the bass; found in similar circumstances, although very rarely, is the augmented triad, usually in its first inversion. (1)

To complete the list the chord of the seventh must be added, with its first and second inversions. Here the dissonant interval must always be prepared.

These harmonic combinations are the result of suspensions:

Authors do not agree about the interpretation of the significance of the harmonies used by the polyphonists. While for some they are no more than the result of the horizontal movement of the voices, and not really harmony as such, for some they perform a definite tonal function, being regarded as the pillars of a bridge, without whose support it could not carry the road running across it.

If the first view is historically correct when speaking of the early centuries of the art of polyphony, it cannot be sustained with regard to the sixteenth century, especially its second half. This was a period of preparation for the change from the modal to the tonal system that took place at the beginning of the seventeenth century with the appearance of the *basso continuo*.

In dealing with the harmonic procedures practised by

G

composers of polyphony, it should be stated that all findings
given here are based on the study of the great masters, the only
ones about whom it is possible to acquire some knowledge
since the others, with some exceptions, are still waiting for their
works to be published. It could happen that these may occasion
surprise, by employing chords not used by the others.

It may not be regarded as especially significant that an
example of an augmented sixth chord can be seen in the Marian
antiphon *Regina caeli laetare* by Guerrero, (2) and that the
combination of G sharp, B flat and D natural is written by
Cardoso in the responsory *Ingrediente Domino*. (3)

In order that these two chords should not be regarded as
examples of far-fetched transcription it can be pointed out
that both composers actually wrote the accidentals changing
the pitch of the altered notes.

COUNTERPOINT

As is well known, the second half of the sixteenth century
represents the apogee of horizontal writing—that is, the art of
composing a piece of music by the interweaving of various
melodies. This is of course why it is called polyphony, or more
accurately, polymelody, a term used nowadays by some authors,
since the former term does not exclude works for groups of
voices conceived vertically.

Seven centuries of peaceful development prepared the
way for the masters of the Renaissance. During this long journey,
various famous craftsmen helped to clear the path later
trod in triumph by Palestrina, Lassus and Victoria. Some
disappeared, leaving no trace of their footprints, others gained
well-merited fame in the history of the art of music—Léonin
and Pérotin, of Paris, in the twelfth century; Philippe de Vitry,
Guillaume de Machaut, Johannes Cesaris, Juan de Cascia,
Girardello Lorenzo, Niccolò da Perugia, Francesco Landino
in the fourteenth century; Johannes de Ciconia, John Dunstable,
Lionel Power, Guillaume Dufay, Gilles Binchois, Jan Ockeg-
hem, Josquin des Prés, Pierre de la Rue, Antoine Brumel, Juan
de Anchieta, Juan Escobar, Francisco de Peñalosa, Lopez de
Baena, Juan del Encina, in the fifteenth century; Adrian
Willaert, Clemens non Papa, Claude Goudimel, Constanza

Festa, Cristóbal de Morales, Giovanni Animuccia and innumerable others in the first half of the sixteenth century.

No attempt will be made to give a detailed study of Renaissance counterpoint; this would be straying too far from the topic under discussion. But brief consideration will be given to the following subjects; *intervals, passing notes, échappées, turns, anticipations, appoggiatures* and *liberties of style.*

Intervals. The story of melodic interval has yet to be told. Nevertheless, in general terms, it can be said that its evolution is characterized by a gradual numerical increase, in ascending order from lesser to greater; the smallest intervals appear first—seconds, thirds, fourths and fifths—sixth and octave coming later.

There is no doubt that Gregorian chant influenced this aspect of polyphony, as it had done modal procedure in earlier centuries.

Within this general trend towards the increasing use of wider intervals, fluctuations and occasional retrogressive tendencies can be seen.

Certain schools, and at times a composer within a particular school, will sacrifice on the altars of a higher aesthetic principle the use of certain intervals employed in former times.

The Roman school is definitely much stricter concerning the use of the intervals of sixth, seventh, ninth and tenth, than the Netherlands school of the fifteenth and early sixteenth centuries.

On the other hand, among the procedures more or less common to a particular style, it can be observed that some composers have a marked preference for certain intervals never used by others.

This is the situation with Victoria in respect of the interval of the diminished fourth, which occurs fairly frequently in his works, while it is rare in those of his contemporaries, Spanish or Italian. (4)

The intervals used most frequently in the sixteenth century are major and minor seconds and thirds, fourths, fifths and octaves. It is rare to find intervals wider than the octave.

Unanimity concerning the use of these intervals does not mean that all composers use them in precisely the same circumstances—on the contrary, with many of them it is a matter of temperament, a question of personal expression rather than syntactical necessity.

It is by examining the essential aspects of the use of the interval of the sixth, more than by any other means, that differences of procedure from one composer to another are most clearly seen.

Thus, Victoria never used the descending interval of the sixth, (5) even as a dead interval, (6) in spite of the fact that, in general terms, his practice was not different from that of his predecessors (7) nor from that of the Palestrinian school.

On the contrary we find, in the works of Victoria, no small percentage of ascending minor sixths, not only as dead intervals, but also, more rarely, as melodic intervals within a phrase. (8)

The situation is the same as far as other composers contemporary with Victoria (9) are concerned.

Of more limited use is the ascending major sixth, although its presence can be shown in the work of many composers. (10)

The reason for this is obscure. It may be that they regarded the sixth as somewhat dissonant and difficult to sing in tune, or possibly it is because of the influence of Gregorian chant, in which it is to be found only exceptionally.

In any case the interval of the sixth, major or minor, is used subject to certain precautions, its unity being broken by means of a caesura interposed between its extremes, depriving it of the strong melodic connection that binds other minor intervals together. Except in rare cases, the notes forming an interval of the sixth are boundaries delimiting neighbouring areas of activity: the end of one phrase or period and the beginning of another.

This characteristic often applies also to the interval of the fifth and, even more so, to that of the octave, as is shown below.

*   *   *   *   *

What is rare in the use of the interval of the sixth is frequent in the case of the octave.

It is very often found as a dead interval, this being appropriate in the case of such a wide interval, but it is no less frequent as a 'live' interval, that is, without any sort of break between its extremities.

In the first case it appears after a cadence, in order to conclude a passage or phrase and begin, at the upper or lower octave, a new theme or a repetition of the preceding one—being much more suitable for this than even the sixth, because of its consonance and greater ease of intonation.

In the second case its use includes very different procedures. Sometimes it forms part of themes made up of notes of long duration; (11) at other times it is found in relatively fast moving melismas; on occasions the first note of the interval is of extremely short duration. (12) As a general rule the leap of an octave is never made by two or more voices simultaneously. Exceptions can however be quoted, as for example in Guerrero's motet *Rorate caeli desuper*. (13)

The use of the octave occurs frequently as a result of expressive or descriptive intentions. Thus the words *terra, descendit* and *suspendit* are set to descending octave leaps; on the other hand *caeli, ascendit* and other words implying height, elevation or growth are expressed by an ascending octave. The example from Guerrero cited above comes under this heading. This demonstrates once more that in the hands of the great masters, the elements of technique are always invested with an artistic significance fully the equal of their basic suitability.

Passing notes. They are absolutely indispensable to florid counterpoint, and accordingly, the polyphonists made special use of them. Sometimes they move by step—this being normal procedure: at others by disjunct movement; frequently they clash against harmony notes; they occur in all voices at once, forming passing chords, or in one at a time; in many cases they produce seventh chords, while in others they create harmonic combinations very difficult to classify. In short, the use of this melodic resource is characterized by the greatest freedom.

As an example we give the use of the passing note running into the unison; this was used much later with great frequency by Bach, but is nevertheless discouraged today by some textbooks on harmony.

Here is a short passage containing a large number of passing notes:

The échappée. This is the name given to a passing note moving by leap of a third. It may be ascending or descending, the latter being much more frequent than the former. (14) At times it occurs in different voices simultaneously, or is used in one voice while another uses stepwise passing notes.

The turn. This is another of the great resources of polyphony, used with considerable freedom. It is used frequently in two or three voices at a time, forming intervals of third and sixth in the first case and complete six–three chords in the second.

mus,   • e -   a -   mus

Anticipations and appoggiaturas. These are melodic devices used less than those listed above, especially appoggiaturas, whose expressive value was not fully realized until a good deal later.

Liberties of Style. Even within a style of writing as perfect as that of the musicians of the Renaissance we find very many liberties of style. These will be listed briefly.

(*a*) *Harmonic liberties.* Direct octaves and fifths are frequent, the actual fifths being separated by notes less in value than a minim or by a short rest; (15) likewise the effect of octaves and perfect fifths, even though those are not incorrect, being found in different voices; (16) fifths produced by passing notes, etc.

(*b*) *Melodic liberties.* Intervals of seventh and even ninth are found, direct or with only one note intervening, and chromatic false relations separated in many cases by notes of very short value; (17) leading notes fall a third instead of rising to the final. (18)

CHAPTER 13

The Themes

Among the materials of construction the themes occupy a most important place because of the impetus they give, throughout its length, to the piece from which they are built, and because its physiognomy and character depend entirely on theirs. Linked closely with the themes is the question of originality, regarded by the polyphonists in quite a different light from that in which it is viewed today.

In this connection it is appropriate to quote Gevaert on the composition of Gregorian melodies:

> While in modern times the composer aims above all at being original, at personally inventing his motifs, each with its own harmony and instrumentation, the Graeco-Roman composers of melodies and later the composers of liturgical cantilenas worked, generally speaking, on traditional themes, from which by means of a process of amplification they obtained new songs. (1)

Actually, the polyphonic composers, in search of themes for their works, had recourse quite frequently to the Gregorian and popular repertories, and even to compositions of their own time or earlier.

On these themes, each with its own particular characteristics, and interspersed with others personally composed, they erect creations which are no less original or expressive in power and force than works based on newly composed material.

Because of their origin, the themes themselves are divided into those borrowed and those personally composed. Both can be either purely melodic or fragments of polyphony. They will be discussed separately.

BORROWED THEMES

MELODIC THEMES

These may be fragments of melodies or complete melodies,

and for purposes of discussion they are classified as follows:

    (*a*) *Cantus firmus 'ostinato'*;

    (*b*) *free cantus firmus.*

(*a*) *Cantus Firmus 'Ostinato'*

This means a melody taken from a Gregorian or popular source which, given in notes of long duration, is like an axis around which the remaining voices of the composition revolve —a pillar about which a luxuriant creeper entwines its magnificent foliage. It is to classical polyphony what it will later become to the organ compositions of Buxtehude, Bach and other composers.

The notes most frequently used to express this sort of theme are the breve and semibreve, dotted or plain, interspersed with minims. Sometimes the written value of each note of the theme remains unaltered through all its repetitions. This is so when the theme is sung with the same words throughout the piece.

On the other hand the written value of the notes will vary when the music of the cantus firmus is adapted to different text-phrases, where the combination of accents and syllables demand different rhythmic forms of the theme.

The *cantus firmus* consists of a single phrase, or at the most a short piece.

In some cases it is entrusted to the same voice from beginning to end of the work; in others it moves from one to another, excluding the bass, as also from one degree of the mode to another, especially from final to dominant, which, apart from avoiding the danger of monotony, provides opportunities for harmonic and cadential variety.

The first notes of the *cantus firmus* give the composer a basis for the construction of the thematic elements, which in their course set the pattern of procedure for the accompanying voices, especially at the beginning of a piece. At other times there is no relationship between these and *cantus firmus*, which then has a role similar to that of the 'canto dado' today in contrapuntal pieces, that is, the other voices are freely invented and not derived from the melodic material of the *cantus firmus*.

Examples of pieces with a *cantus firmus 'ostinato'* are: *Magne Pater Augustine,* for five voices, by Guerrero (2)—the *cantus firmus,* a Gregorian antiphon *Ecce sacerdos magnus,* being repeated

twice, complete; *Andreas Christi famulus*, for five voices, by
Morales, (3) with the *cantus firmus*, *Sancte Andrea*, *ora pro nobis*,
on the tonic and dominant; *Tu es Petrus*, for five voices, by the
same composer, (4) the *cantus firmus*, the phrase *Tu es Petrus*,
alternately on tonic and dominant; *Gaude et laetare Ferrariensis
civitas*, for six voices, by Morales, (5) the *cantus firmus* being
magnificabo nomen tuum in aeternum, on a psalm melody; *Exaltata
est*, for six voices, by Morales, (6) with a *cantus firmus*, *Virgo
prudentissima*, based on the Gregorian melody of that name
on dominant and tonic; *Jubilate Deo omnis terra*, for six voices, by
Morales, (7) here the *cantus firmus*, *Gaudeamus*, on the melody
from the introit of the same name, is on the same note throughout; *Veni, Domine*, for five voices, by Esquivel, (8) the *cantus
firmus*, *Veni, Domine et noli tardare* being alternately on tonic and
dominant.

In all these compositions the *cantus firmus* is repeated with
unaltered rhythm, and each repetition is separated from the
preceding one by the same number of rests.

Missa Gaudeamus, for six voices, by Victoria, (9) provides an
example of *cantus firmus* 'ostinato' in which, from the beginning
of the *Gloria*, the note values change with each repetition,
because of the different length of the phrases of text to which
it is adapted.

A typical example of *cantus firmus* 'ostinato' is the motet *O lux
et decus Hispaniae*, by Infantas (10)—the *cantus firmus* consists
of the phrase *O lux et decus Hispaniae, sanctissime Jacobe* given
three times, but the second statement, beginning on the second
degree of the mode while the others begin on the first, is an
inversion of the intervals of the theme, that is to say, ascending
intervals become descending intervals and vice versa.

(b) Free Cantus Firmus
As in the previous case it is a Gregorian melody and there are
various types of treatment, the most frequent being those given
below:

(i) *Complete melodies*. The polyphonic composers frequently
take a complete Gregorian melody—a hymn, an antiphon or a
psalm tone. The composer respects the structure , at the most
breaking it by short rests between its various parts. Each of these

parts—verses in the hymns, half-versicles in the psalm tones—is clothed in a garment of imitative counterpoint, whose generating motifs are derived in some cases from the same Gregorian tune while in others they bear no relationship to it.

The plan of the work thus created depends entirely on the form of the theme on which it is based. This undergoes a more or less extensive process of re-touching at the hands of the composer. Sometimes he lengthens the note values, sometimes he shortens them, on occasion he omits notes he considers superfluous, at times he decorates the theme or extends it in the cadences with the idea of achieving a more satisfactory conclusion. In a sentence the composer treats the *cantus firmus* freely from a personal point of view, making it conform to his own ideas concerning rhythm.

He does, however, respect the melodic outlines of the theme so that it is easily discernible within the texture of the accompanying voices.

As a general rule the cantus firmus is entrusted to the top voice, though there are numerous cases in which each phrase in turn is given to a different voice in the polyphonic texture, thus giving life and energy to the whole.

From the point of view of rhythm there are two clearly distinguishable methods of treating these themes. In the first the notes of the Gregorian melody are lengthened considerably, each note of the theme being given as a breve or semibreve (and occasionally longer), a procedure which could be considered as expressive of a state of ecstasy, being used a good deal in requiem masses; in the second, the Gregorian melody assumes a rhythmic aspect very different from the preceding one, notes shorter than a breve being used, as a general rule, in its interpretation.

Examples of works composed on complete melodies are *Missa pro defunctis*, for four voices, by Victoria; (11) *Jesu Redemptor omnium*, for four equal voices, by the same composer; (12) *Crudelis Herodes*, for four voices, by Guerrero; (13) *Veni Creator*, for four voices, by Guerrero (14)—with the Gregorian melody in the *tenor* in the first strophe, in the *cantus* in the second, and in *cantus secundus* in the third; *Benedictus, Dominus Deus Israel*, for four voices, by Ortiz (15)—the first mode melody appearing sometimes in one voice and sometimes in another;

Estote fortes in bello, for four voices by Victoria; (16) *Virgo prudentissima* for four voices by Infantas (17) with the Gregorian melody, barely discernible, moving from one voice to another. Infantas has a long list of motets composed on appropriate Gregorian melodies (18) as also has Juan Vásquez in his *Agenda defunctorum*. (19)

(ii) *Fragmented melodies*. At times the polyphonists take a Gregorian melody and break it up according to their fancy, in a somewhat arbitrary fashion, into various small fragments, making each one a corner-stone of the different parts of a musical edifice. This procedure was used in the composition of masses.

Thus the mass *Ave maris stella*, for four voices, by Victoria, has for its theme the tune of the hymn from which it takes its name.

Victoria composed the first *Kyrie* on the music of the first line of the hymn; the first two statements of *Christe eleison* take as their starting point the three first notes of the second line, and then, in the third and fourth statements of *Christe eleison* the melody of the third line is sung in long notes, leaving the verse unfinished here, to begin the second *Kyrie* with another statement of the first phrase of the hymn, which, in the final *Kyrie eleison*, refers back to the third line.

The *Gloria* is designed in the same way, the music of the fourth line appearing for the first time in its *Amen*.

(iii) *Melodic beginnings*. Sometimes the polyphonists give the impression of being like birds who cannot start flying except from a point some distance above the ground. They need a spring-board from which to soar aloft on wings of inspiration, and this is provided by the Gregorian melodies. The composers use the first notes to get started, moving independently once they are under way.

Missa de Beata Virgine for four voices, by Morales (20) will serve as an example. Morales takes for his theme in the *Kyries* the melody of mass IX—*cum jubilo*—of the *Kyriale*.

He uses the first eight notes of the *Kyrie* to get his polyphony moving, later abandoning the liturgical theme to make his own way. He uses the first statement of *Christe eleison* in composing his own, and the last seven notes of the last *Kyrie* as a starting point for the second *Kyrie* of his mass.

On the same theme, used in the same way, Victoria composed the *Kyries* of his *Missa de Beata Virgine*. (21)

As has already been pointed out several times, the composers of polyphony made use of secular themes in the composition of their works, a custom which was forbidden by the Council of Trent.

Each composer chose the secular song he favoured or the one most widely known in his locality. But there was one tune used by almost all the composers of polyphony from the fifteenth to well into the seventeenth century—*L'homme armé*, a favourite of Charles V. Even the austere Morales used this in the compostion of two masses. (22)

POLYPHONIC THEMES

The foregoing paragraphs have dealt with pieces composed on melodies.

Apart from these procedures, used as we have seen in the composition of all kinds of music, the polyphonists made use of another practice, almost exclusively in masses.

It consists of making use of portions of a motet or a song written by either the composer himself or by some other composer, in the composition of a mass—hence the name Parody mass.

The different sections of the motet are used in different parts of the mass, sometimes with no other modifications than those required by the new text, but in other cases, by contrast, adapted extensively by the composer, this producing a genuine variation of the original.

The composer does not always make use of the fragments of the motet in their entirety—sometimes he appropriates only one or two voices, the others being newly composed.

Although it is true that the first bars of the motet are frequently found as the beginning of the *Kyrie*, they can also be found in other parts of the mass. In the same way the remaining fragments of the model are transferred from one part of the mass to another, and are incorporated, sometimes at the beginning, sometimes halfway through or perhaps at the end of the *Gloria, Credo, Sanctus* or *Agnus Dei*.

This procedure was used extensively by all the polyphonists, even the most prolific. Of the eighteen masses extant by Victoria, to quote one example, seven are composed on his own motets. These bear the following titles, corresponding to the motets on which they are based—*Quam pulchri sunt*, (23) *O quam gloriosum est regnum*, (24) *O magnum mysterium*, (25) *Trahe me post te*, (26) *Ascendens Christus*, (27) *Dum complerentur* (28) and *Vidi speciosam*. (29)

The connection between the Parody mass and the related motet is not the same in all compositions—it varies from piece to piece, and composer to composer; that is to say, the polyphonists did not conform to a set pattern of procedure; rather they allowed themselves the greatest freedom in the use they made of the model.

ORIGINAL THEMES

In the study of original themes, distinction must be made between, on the one hand, masses, hymns and psalms, or strictly liturgical pieces, and on the other hand motets, whose text in many instances is taken from the liturgy, but in many others is freely sought by the composer in various places, especially in the books of the Bible. Certainly both are sacred— but the former belong more properly to divine worship than the latter.

Thus it is clear that the polyphonists, in composing these pieces, may find their imagination bound by principles of a higher order, principles to which they bow with becoming humility. Because of this, these works permit only very limited encounter with the idiosyncrasies of expression found in freely composed themes.

On the other hand, the motets less dedicated to a liturgical purpose—even in many cases quite legitimately secular—allow their composers a freer and more personal expression of their creative powers. The opportunity of selecting texts to suit their own taste ensures perfect agreement between the subject of the piece and the inner aspirations of the soul. It is here, conse- quently, that we find a limitless range of shades of expression, an echo of the inner music of the heart.

The influence of the text in the construction of thematic

motifs is two-fold—first in connection with its content, and secondly in its grammatical form.

In the first case the composer may feel himself impelled to represent the meaning of the text symbolically, in a special way, by means of the direction and pitch of the sounds, when the words of the phrase contain ideas of movement and dimension.

Innumerable examples can be quoted, among them the motet *Ascendens Christus in altum*, for five voices, by Victoria. (30) The ascending form of the motif, which, in addition, moves through the range of an octave, represents the ascension of Christ on high. A similar instance is found in *Rorate caeli desuper*, by Guerrero. (31) Here also the words *caeli* and *desuper* suggested to the composer the ascending direction of the theme, while the phrase *aperiatur terra* in the same piece is represented musically by the low tessitura in which the composer places all the voices at that point. Palestrina has done the same thing in the phrase *in caelo et in terra* from the offertory *Laudate Dominum*, for five voices. (32) Guerrero makes use of an arpeggiated chord with the idea of imitating the sound of a trumpet in the theme of *Canite tuba in Sion*, (33) a procedure which Palestrina also employs on the word *buccinate* in the motet *Exsultate Deo* for five voices. (34) These examples also express ideas of dimension.

If the text contains ideas of movement the polyphonists resort, for its symbolic expression, to notes of short duration. This is done by Palestrina on the word *obviaverunt* in his *Pueri Hebraeorum*; (35) and by Victoria on the word *gressus* in the motet *Quam pulchri sunt*, (36) and on *eamus* in *Magi viderunt stellam*; (37) so also Guerrero on the words *et venerunt festinantes*, in his *Pastores loquebantur* for six voices. (38)

In all these cases a melodic thematic motif suddenly appears, expressed in the smallest note-values, with the obvious intention of reflecting the idea contained in the verbal phrase.

In addition to the examples quoted, many other associations of ideas are found in the polyphonists. There are the ascending scales used by Victoria and Esquivel on the word *Gaudent* in their respective motets *O quam gloriosum est regnum*, for four voices. These are very clearly intended to express flexibly in sound the joy of the saints in glory. More original is the sinuous, tortuous movement adopted by Luca Marenzio on the word *serpente*, with which he achieves a perfect imitation of this reptile's gliding motion. (39)

Certainly innumerable examples can be quoted, covering a wide range of shades of expression evoked by the composers by means of sound pictures of very diverse colouring.

It is important to point out here that this pictorial-descriptive tendency in the themes of the motet was influenced decisively by the style of the madrigal, which was extraordinarily rich in inflections, accents and colours.

The relationship between the grammatical construction of the text and the structure of the motifs is not easy to establish because in many cases we do not know for certain the right way to fit the text to the music. It can only be asserted that, from the study of the works of Lassus, Palestrina, Victoria, Guerrero, Castro and other composers who follow faithfully the rules of Zarlino concerning the underlaying of text, the following can be established: preference for placing the accented syllable in relief by means of one of the following procedures—matching it with the melismas within the phrases or with notes of longer duration or higher pitch than those given to unaccented syllables.

TEXT AND RHYTHM

The influence of text on the music does not end with those aspects of it studied above. In addition, it rules the greater rhythm as well as creating the lesser rhythm, the rhythm of detail.

It is very difficult to talk of rhythm in classical polyphony, as the views of the polyphonists themselves concerning rhythm are not known. The writers of treatises do not mention this topic, even in passing. In each case they only discuss the bar, the methods of indicating it, and the notes that comprise it. Did they identify one with the other? That can be answered today with a categorical 'no'. The rhythm is independent of the bar; the rhythm cuts across the bar, beginning where the bar concludes and finishing where it begins.

The rhythm definitely is not the bar, and even less is this the case in polyphonic music, since here the bar, as it is understood today, does not exist; polyphony knew nothing of the restrictive grouping of notes between bar-lines, nor of the theory of the strong and weak parts of the bar.

Polyphony has its origin in Gregorian chant and it is logical, therefore, that it should have the same or apparently the same natural rhythm. There is order in the movement certainly, because without order there is no rhythm: but this order is not determined by any sort of regularly recurring pattern.

The rhythm of polyphony is an undulating movement, rising and falling according to the requirements of the verbal text. Grammatical logic is the factor governing the greater musical rhythm of polyphony: and so the literary text is included among the materials of construction.

But the text exercises its influence not only in the creation of the greater rhythm of the phrase; the lesser rhythm, the rhythmic detail, derives from the physiognomy of the lesser units of the verbal phrase, namely the words. Depending on whether they have their accent on the penultimate or ante-penultimate syllable, they can create binary or ternary rhythms within the greater rhythm.

From this it follows that in a piece written in a binary time-signature, ternary rhythms appear frequently, produced by the particular accentuation of words with accents on the ante-penultimate syllable, and vice versa.

Particularly graphic examples, universally known, among the innumerable examples that could be quoted, are the phrase *suspendimus organa nostra*, from Palestrina's motet *Super flumina Babylonis*, for four voices, (40) and the words *surgite, surgite* from the responsory, *Una hora* by Victoria. (41)

The simultaneous articulation of words whose accents fall in different places gives polyphonists an opportunity to create simultaneous binary and ternary rhythms. Palestrina has a magnificent example in the offertory *Laudate Dominum*, for five voices; the words *psallite nomini ejus* provide a fine combination of contrasting rhythms. (42)

Putting on one side this contrast of rhythms created by the combination of words the accents of which may fall in different places, it must be stated quite definitely, as a general principle, that polyphonic music is essentially polyrhythmic because it is polymelodic. Each voice is a melody with its own rhythmic pattern, the verbal text (as has been said earlier) being the

H

factor governing, both in general character and in detail, the ebb and flow of the rhythmic movement.

This action of the text on the rhythm is shown whenever the polyphonists write a homophonic passage: the accents dominate the musical situation, imposing their authority on all the other elements which combine to create the different melodies making up the polyphonic whole.

But the influence of the text does not reach its limit here; it is seen in the metrical division of the rhythmic values.

It is interesting to observe how different composers use the same rhythmic pattern for the words of a phrase they set to music, for example, the phrase *dona nobis pacem, Dominus Deus Sabaoth, Gratias agimus tibi*, etc. of the mass. Others, instead of conforming to a single rhythmic pattern, use three or four, very similar to each other.

CHAPTER 14

Organization of the
Complete Polyphonic Fabric

The materials of construction studied in previous chapters are, apart from chords, melodic in character. In theory these chords only result from the forming of melodies, that is to say, in the spinning of the separate threads which form part of the polyphonic texture.

A further step forward in the study of the polyphonic forms will make it possible to see how the composer interweaves different strands of melody in the creation of a piece of polyphony, which can be defined in essence as the simultaneous combination of different melodies.

The organization of the whole polyphonic fabric of a work comprises three stages—the beginning of the piece, its central portion and its conclusion.

THE BEGINNING

1. *The opening imitations*

The voices in a piece may make their entry in two ways— together or one after the other.

In the first case the contrapuntal procedure called homophony will result. This will be discussed later on. In the second case each voice as it appears on the scene usually repeats with greater or lesser exactness the theme sung by those preceding it. These are known as imitations.

The voice announcing the theme is called the antecedent, the subject, *dux* or *propuesta*; the voice which replies is called the consequent, the answer or *comes*.

The imitation is *regular* when the answer reproduces exactly the intervals of the subject; that is to say, when a major third in the theme is answered by a major third in reply to it, when a

99

minor second is answered by a minor second, etc.; it is irregular whenever the intervals of answer and subject do not correspond exactly.

The answer may be *real* or *tonal*. The first consists of a transposition of the theme a fifth higher, so that if the subject begins on C the answer will begin on G, the intervals being reproduced exactly. The answer is *tonal* when the subject moves from final to dominant or vice versa, the intervening notes being adjusted or altered as required.

Having defined these terms, let us examine the situation in classical polyphony.

Irregular imitations occur quite frequently; moreover, within the same piece the answers are sometimes regular and sometimes irregular, as for example in the first fourteen bars of the motet *Canite tuba* by Guerrero. (1)

Thus, both real and tonal answers are commonly used, although the latter are perhaps more frequent, especially when the themes are taken from the Gregorian repertory, to whose exigencies this procedure conforms most readily.

The intervals preferred in answering are the octave, fifth and fourth. Rarely are any others used, although in the fifteenth century the third was in frequent use, and even in the sixteenth century it is used by Lassus and occasionally by others.

Although it does not happen often it is possible to quote examples of imitation by contrary motion. As a small sample the motet *Benedicta filia* by Infantas (2) may be studied, this serving at the same time as an example of imitation at the third.

Seen as a whole the beginning of a polyphonic piece in imitative style is, in its form, very similar to a plain fugue exposition. Each voice states either subject or answer. This exposition is repeated, the composer modifying the order of appearance of subject and answer, the entries of the voices, the accompanying counterpoint and even the rhythmic contour of the theme.

Examples

(*a*) Plain single exposition—*Juxta vestibulum et altare*, for four voices by Ceballos, (3) the subject being in *cantus* answered by *altus*, then in *tenor* answered by *bassus*.

(*b*) Double exposition—*Ecce nunc tempus* for four voices by Guerrero. (4) Here the subject is in *tenor* and *cantus* at the octave, the answer being in *altus* and *bassus*. In the repetition the subject is in *cantus* and the answer in *bassus* while the other two voices have new accompanying motifs, and *tenor* restates the subject at the beginning of the last phrase of this exposition. Further examples are *Magi viderunt stellam* for four voices by Victoria, (5) and *Canite tuba in Sion* for four voices, by Guerrero, (6) the theme of this motet being an example of rhythmic variation.

The exposition of the opening theme concludes with a modulating cadence which prepares for the appearance of the second episode, as will be shown below.

Within this general pattern of procedure for the opening imitations of a piece, there is room for innumerable variations of procedure, not only between different composers, but within the work of a single composer.

2. *The order of entry of the voices*

Discussion will be confined to compositions for four voices, this being the most common grouping as well as the easiest to study.

There are no fixed rules concerning the order in which the voices in a piece should enter—the composer decides this in each case according to the characteristics of the theme, and taking into account the effect he wishes to obtain.

All who have made a study of fugal writing are well aware of the different gradation of sound that can be achieved according to whether the voices make their appearance in order from high to low, or vice versa.

In both cases the same quantitative effect results, the cumulative total of four elements gradually increasing the volume of sound. But the qualitative result is very different. While the entry of the voices in order from low to high in pitch produces the sensation of a progressive increase of vital energy, the inverse order suggests a loss of tension in interpretation.

This being so it is obvious that these details could not have been overlooked by the polyphonists, almost all of whom were choirmasters, and in every case superlative craftsmen in the art of counterpoint.

With four voices twenty-four different orders of entry are possible:

1	CATB	7	ACTB	13	TCAB	19	BCAT
2	CABT	8	ACBT	14	TCBA	20	BCTA
3	CTAB	9	ATCB	15	TACB	21	BACT
4	CTBA	10	ATBC	16	TABC	22	BATC
5	CBAT	11	ABCT	17	TBCA	23	BTCA
6	CBTA	12	ABTC	18	TBAC	24	BTAC

In the use of these combinations it is possible to observe, across the centuries, a process of elimination of those less suitable for the formation of balanced sonorous periods.

Thus, while composers of the fifteenth and early sixteenth centuries begin a work with the simultaneous or successive entry of the two outer voices (CB or BC) the masters of the Roman school take great care to avoid these groupings because of the strong contrast of light and shade produced, or (in musical terms) because of the distance between the two voices, with its resulting disequilibrium and lack of blend.

It is for this reason that the combinations numbered 5, 6, 19, 20 are not found in the whole of Victoria's work.

The disappointingly small number of editions available prevents a detailed study of this aspect of the technique of imitation. A reading of the complete works of Palestrina and Victoria, however, and of those of other composers published in various collections, makes it possible for us to establish the following principles about the order of entry of the voices, at least in the works of the polyphonic composers of the Roman school.

(*a*) Whenever the subject is stated by one of the outer voices the answer is given in one of the inner parts.

(*b*) Symmetrical combinations seem to be preferred, TBCA, CATB, CTAB, ATCB, etc.

(*c*) For preference, the entry of the lowest voice is delayed till last. (7)

3. *Tonal connection between the first note of the theme and the concluding chord of the piece*

The tonal awareness of each composer is revealed in a special way in the choice of the first note of the first theme of a composition.

As a general rule the first note of a theme is in the relationship of octave, fifth or fourth with the bass note of the final chord of the piece, this being at the same time in most cases the final.

This tonal relationship between the beginning and end of a work must have become established as normal in the second half of the sixteenth century. Such composers as Josquin des Prés and Willaert often work quite differently.

In fact the great polyphonists of this period always sought a close relationship between the beginning and end of each piece. This is true even of composers who may, in some ways, appear somewhat primitive, such as Morales.

Of course, this procedure applies only to personally composed themes. If, on the other hand, the themes come from the Gregorian repertory, the composer cannot, in many cases, establish this tonal relationship, since, as is well known, many Gregorian melodies begin on notes forming the interval of second or third with their final.

Cases can be quoted in which the composer did venture to modify the beginning of the Gregorian melody in order to obtain this tonal relationship between the beginning and end of a piece.

Such an instance, among others, is *Lauda Sion*, for four voices, by Palestrina, (8) composed on the melody of the sequence of that name. The composer replaces the initial note E by D, the fifth of the chord on the final.

4. *The chords formed by entry of the voices*

When the second voice makes its appearance a consonant interval is produced, with almost exclusive preference for the perfect consonances, fifth, octave or unison. The polyphonists never resort to dissonance to emphasize the entry of the second voice.

It is a regular procedure in some composers—for example Palestrina and Victoria—for the entry of the third voice to make, with the voices already sounding, a complete triad. To achieve this Victoria does not scruple, if necessary, to introduce an alteration in his thematic motif. Accordingly, in the motet *Resplenduit facies ejus, altus* replaces the thematic leap of the fifth by that of a third, so that at the entry of *cantus secundus* the chord sounding will be G–B flat–D, not G–D.

At the entry of the fourth voice it is usual to have a complete triad with the bass note doubled. On rare occasions the third or fifth may be doubled or a six–four or seventh chord used.

ORGANIZATION OF THE POLYPHONIC FABRIC DURING THE COURSE OF A COMPOSITION

1. *The exposition of new themes*

The exposition of the opening theme concludes with a cadence —sometimes obvious, sometimes not—a cadence which prepares the second theme in the way discussed below.

Generally speaking, each new theme differs entirely from its predecessors, so that the composer can exercise his creative power during a piece just as many times as there are episodes in the text he wishes to set. Nevertheless he subordinates the importance of these to the first theme.

This is the door of the cathedral, and for that reason it is more impressive. The others are interior columns of the temple which do not leap into view in quite the same way, this being why, in many cases, they lack distinctive features. The composer handles these with greater freedom—he extends some by the addition of little melismas, while shortening others by omitting notes—imitations differ from their source through modifications made in the intervals—he subjects them to rhythmic variations, metrical displacements (9) and numberless other adjustments which cannot be discussed in detail in a few words.

From the point of view of imitation, as a general principle, the themes appearing during the course of a piece are treated in the same or a similar manner as the first. It should be pointed out, however, that sometimes there is more repetition of themes at certain points, sometimes for one voice, sometimes for others with the idea of emphasizing an especially important phrase; that, while at the beginning all voices have either subject or answer, all voices do not take part in some imitations; and finally that there are partial imitations, or imitations which reproduce not the whole but only a part of their model, or which omit some interval or some of its most characteristic aspects.

It is clear that these circumstances arise at times in the exposition of the opening theme. Thus, in the motet *Domine non sum dignus* by Victoria, the two upper voices do not take part in the imitation of the beginning of the theme but begin with the words *non sum dignus*.

To maintain interest, or perhaps as a way of treating intermediate phrases, the polyphonists made use of harmonico-contrapuntal progressions in which sometimes all voices take part, while in other cases only some participate. A good example of this technique is provided by the phrase *ut intres sub tectum meum* of the above-mentioned motet by Victoria. The second phrase, *ut intres*, repeats the music of the preceding passage a third lower, with slight variations introduced in the second voice.

It should be made clear, however, that the polyphonists of the sixteenth century, aware of the ease with which it is possible for the use of progressions to degenerate into routine procedure, use them with great economy and always with masterly judgment.

2. *Transition from one theme to another*

One of the most essential things in polyphony is the continuous flow of melody, the unbroken progression of sound in motion. No piece of polyphony can be regarded as a series of passages bounded by their respective cadences and separated one from another by a rest, however short—nothing could be more out of keeping with the art of polyphony.

With this necessity for continuous movement there must be combined another factor no less essential to polyphony, the obvious contrast between the different passages (no matter how short) which, taken together, comprise the whole.

For this reason the polyphonists felt themselves obliged to seek a compromise with the idea of reconciling, without loss to either, these two opposing elements in polyphony: the continuity of sound in motion and the reasonable demarcation between the different sections of a work, demarcation which does not break down its unity but does make its formal structure clearer.

To achieve this, a tremendous evolutionary progress can be seen in the second half of the sixteenth century. If we compare the works of this period with those of the preceding century, it will be noted that in the fifteenth-century composers it is often very difficult to determine where one phrase ends and the following phrase begins. In other words the reluctance to interrupt the flow of sound was the reason why composers were not particularly concerned with clear definition of phrases and passages within a greater unity. But composers of the sixteenth century brought the reconciling of these two requirements of polyphony to a very fine art.

The cadences are the key to the solution of this problem, the place where this rapprochement occurs. The cadences conclude the exposition of each theme, like stones marking the boundaries of neighbouring fields—but at the same time they are like a bridge between the banks of a river, without whose help it is impossible to cross from one side to the other.

If at the end of the cadence all the voices come to a halt, even for a brief moment, interruption of melodic continuity has occurred, in opposition (as has already been pointed out several times) to the real nature of polyphony. If occasionally composers do this, it is to obtain a particular effect and is an exception. On the other hand, if in the cadence some voices come to a halt while others continue their movement, the cadential effect has been achieved while the continuity of sound has not suffered in any way. Even one voice on its own is enough to ensure this continuity.

The best ways of maintaining movement from one theme to another are these:

(*a*) One voice concludes the phrase some time before the others, and rests briefly. While the remaining voices complete the cadence, the voice that was resting makes its entry on one of the concluding chords, almost always the penultimate, stating the theme of the following phrase in whose exposition the others take part as it continues.

Bars 25–27 of Victoria's motet *O magnum mysterium* (10) serve as an example. *Bassus* is resting from half way through bar 25, through bar 26 and for the first three-quarters of bar 27. In the concluding part of this—the penultimate chord of the cadence being formed by the other voices—*bassus* enters with the new theme of the phrase *jacentem in praesepio*.

Victoria: 'O magnum mysterium'

This procedure admits of countless variations as can be seen by anyone who cares to examine different polyphonic pieces for himself. But it is always essentially the same: the voice or voices which are resting may do this for long or short periods: sometimes it will add up to bars, as in the example given above, sometimes it will only be part of a bar. Thus in bar 30 of the motet *Canite tuba in Sion* (11) the second voice announces the theme of the phrase *ad salvandum nos* after a rest of only part of a bar. The composer makes the voices rest, now one, now others, according to whether he wishes to create a weaker or stronger feeling of repose. Equally, the object of these procedures is always the same—to ensure on the one hand the continuous flow of the music, and on the other to define, without separating, the various sections of a work.

(*b*) At other times all the voices articulate the final syllable of a phrase at the same time, one or two of them beginning the new melodic motif in the latter part of the bar, while the others sustain the chord for some time. For example, in the third bar of *Miserere mei*, (12) the second part of the motet *Domine non sum dignus* by Victoria, the four voices conclude the plagal cadence simultaneously; but while the first and third sustain the notes of the chord the other two announce the next theme.

Here is another example, from the *Sanctus* of *Missa Quam pulchri sunt*, by Victoria:

3. *Canonic imitations*

To ensure consistency throughout all the polyphonic fabric from beginning to end of the composition, composers not infrequently make use of the procedure known as *canonic imitation*. This consists of a continuous melody, freely composed, sung by two or more voices at different intervals of the scale, fourth, fifth, octave and also unison.

This contrapuntal device, used in all sorts of pieces, was obligatory in the third *Agnus Dei* in masses, in the final verse of the *Magnificat* and in the doxology of hymns.

The ease with which the polyphonists avoid the tremendous difficulties posed by the composition of canons is most impressive, and more remarkable still is the spirit which they succeed in infusing into them. This makes it abundantly clear that technical devices have a purpose other than the pleasure of solving a problem, or the desire of the composer to demonstrate his skill.

The canon is not a device having no connection with the other voices; it is on the contrary, their centre of gravity; it gives them significance, unity and value, at the same time supporting them like the arches of a building. Frequently the voices not taking part in the canonic imitation still derive their essential character from it, and in spite of forming with it a single unified whole, they are not deprived of their individuality, though they are not completely independent.

As examples the following pieces can be studied—*Ave Virgo*, for five voices, by Guerrero; (13) *Crudelis Herodes* (the fourth strophe) by the same composer; (14) *Ave Maria*, for five voices, by Morales; (15) *Veni Creator* by Guerrero, (16) the last strophe; *Magnificat* by Guerrero, (17) the last verse; *Magnificat* by Victoria, (18) the last verse; *Magnificat* by Aguilera de Heredia, (19) the last verse. Victoria has a quadruple canon in the third *Agnus Dei*, for eight voices, from *Missa Simile est regnum caelorum*. (20)

ORGANIZATION OF THE CONCLUSION OF A PIECE

The polyphonic organization of the final section of the composition makes use of the same procedure as those preceding it—a theme presented in imitative style, but concluding with a definitive, not a provisional cadence, as in all the earlier sections.

In exceptional cases there are elaborate final sections based on an interlinked series of progressions. A curious example can be seen in the *Alleluia* of the motet *Surrexit Pastor bonus* (21) by R. Coloma.

The following points are worth noting in connection with the final section:

(*a*) Polyphonists frequently give greater fullness to the exposition of the closing theme. This doubtless fulfils the requirements of formal equilibrium, which needs a well-rounded final section, not an abruptly-ended flow of movement.

The exposition of the last phrase of the motet *Juxta vestibulum et altare* by Ceballos (22) should be compared with that of the preceding phrases. While the longest of these does not exceed eleven bars, the last phrase is fifteen bars in length. It is quite clear that this is a real consideration. Classical polyphony, more than any other art, does not consort happily with any kind of rigid formalism.

(*b*) Harmonically the cadence is formed by these progressions V–I, V being preceded sometimes by IV or IV^{6}_{5}; in place of V–I the plagal cadence (IV–I) is frequently used. After the progression V–I composers often organize a short coda of three or four bars, sometimes imitative in style, sometimes homophonic. Here, one of the voices sustains its note like a pedal while the others elaborate a harmonic pattern, moving in turn to the degrees IV–I or IV–I⁶–IV–I. The object of this coda, obviously, is to give complete and final confirmation of the Perfect cadence V–I, thus creating the impression of a smooth and quiet conclusion at the end of the work.

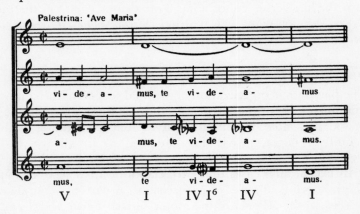

HOMOPHONY

In this chapter the organization of the entire polyphonic fabric in the imitative style has been discussed. But there still remains another procedure no less frequent in use and no less expressive. This is homophony, or the art of composing a passage in note-against-note counterpoint, which excludes almost everything ornamental in character.

Although it is not strictly proper in connection with the period under discussion, this procedure can be compared with the vertical harmonization of a melody as against the imitative contrapuntal style, the essence of which is the horizontal line.

This style, commonly used for many years previously in the composition of longer parts of the mass such as the *Gloria* and especially the *Credo*, was accepted quite definitely by the polyphonists of the Roman school and their associates, not only in the pieces referred to above, but in all others, especially the motet. Here there is a constant opposition between the two types of musical texture—florid-imitative counterpoint and note-against-note counterpoint.

What is more, it can be affirmed that the imitative-linear style, peculiar to earlier periods and especially to the Netherlands school, underwent in the second half of the sixteenth century a process of evolution in the direction of the homophonic style, obviously without abandoning the melodic independence of the voices.

It should not be assumed that this technique was, in the hands of the composers, merely a means of avoiding monotony or producing effects of contrast. Rather it should be affirmed that when the masters did make use of it they did so for a highly expressive purpose—further corroboration of the fact that these composers never relied on technique for its own sake, but used it as the humble servant of inspiration.

The most frequent uses of homophony will be listed briefly:

(*a*) In expressing thoughts and ideas of admiration, adoration and supplication. Everyone knows the typical case in the motets of Victoria known by the 'O' of the opening exclamation of the text—*O Regem caeli!*, *O sacrum convivium!*, *O quam gloriosum est regnum!*, and many others.

(*b*) In expressing happiness, rejoicing and similar ideas. Who does not recall the motet *Exultate justi*, by Viadana; (23) the *alleluias* from *O Regem caeli!*, and *O magnum mysterium!* by Victoria, or the phrase *et sanabitur anima mea* from *Domine non sum dignus* by the same composer?

(*c*) With the idea of achieving an increase of sonority in the concluding section of a composition, or to express ideas of strength, power, grandeur, etc. In this last connection we must quote the words *Deus, fortis* from the motet *Ecce virgo concipiet* by Morales. (24)

The citing of examples in these three cases has been intentionally sparing because they are so numerous that we assume they are within reach of all.

CHAPTER 15

The Set Musical Forms of
Polyphony

THE MOTET

In actual fact it is not possible to speak of different polyphonic forms in the sense of each liturgical piece being constructed in its own particular way, as happened in later centuries with, for example, the fugue, the sonata, the minuet, etc.

From the point of view of form there is no difference between the various polyphonic pieces in the liturgy. If we are shown a motet, a strophe of a hymn, a verse of a *Magnificat* and a *Kyrie* from a mass, without their text, the only discernible difference between them is the purely external one that some are longer or shorter than others.

As far as their internal construction is concerned, it is not possible to indicate any significant differences, and unless it is composed around a *cantus firmus* no one will be able to say, with certainty, which of the four pieces is the motet, the mass, the hymn or the *Magnificat*.

This is due to the fact that in the sixteenth century musical composition conformed to a single principle of construction, applied in exactly the same way in all pieces—masses, hymns, motets, psalms, lessons, responsories. This principle is known today as *motet style* or *motet procedure*, because it is exemplified and attains its greatest perfection in the composition of that name.

(a) Its origin and evolution

The word *motet* is, according to Aubry (*Cent Motets du XIIIe siècle*, Paris, 1908, p. 17), the diminutive form of the word *mot*, which both in French and Provençal signifies a poem, just as *son* indicates in the same languages a song. This diminutive, coined to describe a short piece, was taken over into Latin as *motetus*, used frequently in various thirteenth-century texts and persisting in the title of some sixteenth-century editions alongside the more common form *motecta*.

This word was applied to a musical form when in the performance of a pre-existing piece a text different from the original was adapted to it syllabically; when later the number of voices was increased to three, the *duplum* or voice adjacent to the *tenor* was still called *motet*; this term coming, through usage, to mean the whole composition.

Musically the motet derives from the *organa* practised in the school of Nôtre Dame at the end of the twelfth and the beginning of the thirteenth century. Pérotin had written, in the style of the *organum*, some compositions called *clausulae*, to alternate with the Gregorian melodies of the proper of the mass and the office, phrases built on a Gregorian fragment, this serving as their support while at the same time retaining its own text. The upper voices of these miniature pieces were genuine vocalizations, being made up musically of magnificent melismas, with the text limited to articulating the same vowel as in the words being sung by the *tenor*. Realizing the beauty of these small-scale creations, composers decided to fit to the melodic graces of the upper part a syllabic Latin text, the *tenor* retaining in his part the proper liturgical text. And thus was born the motet, whose essence, according to the mediaeval theorists, is the singing of different texts at the same time.

According to this the motet is not an original creation, an invention of a particular date; its origin is due to a further step made by *organum* as it evolved. The origin of the motet is sacred; it is born within the purest liturgical atmosphere, even if, in a later period as will be shown presently, it deviates from this line and admits between its staves texts far from liturgical.

The evolution of the motet is one of the most interesting studies in the history of music, and it can be discussed under as few as three headings—number of voices, text and rhythm.

The number of voices increased progressively from two to three, the last being called *triplum*. As a rule the two upper voices sung the same text, in opposition to the *cantus firmus* which preserved its independence, both rhythmic and textual. The liturgical themes used in the motet were extremely varied, antiphons, alleluias, sequences, tropes, responsories, etc.

I

During a later phase, whose date cannot be determined precisely, a text in the vernacular was fitted to the *duplum* of the motet, the *tenor* still retaining the Gregorian melody with its corresponding liturgical words. These new texts were not always religious in character—they often degenerated into love songs (when not irreverent or even lewd), against which various bishops and ecclesiastical writers raised their voices during the later years of the thirteenth century, when the motet attained an extraordinary development and widespread use. Finally Pope John XXII put a stop to this and other abuses that had been introduced into music with his memorable *Docta sanctorum Patrum*, a bull published in 1324.

At the end of the thirteenth century the *triplum* achieved its independence from the *duplum* in the matter of text, the result being a tri-textual motet.

As far as rhythm is concerned, it is necessary to remember the following facts in order to understand the development of the motet from this point of view. The *tenor* of the first forms of polyphony—*organum*, *diaphony* and *discantus*—followed the rhythm of the principal voice; but little by little the artistic instinct of the composers forced them to ignore the restrictions which obliged both voices to move in step. And so it came about that they invented the rhythmic schemes known as modes, derived from classical metre.

Pérotin and his school give to the top voices of the *clausulae* one of these rhythms, this being respected faithfully by the composers who later made them into motets. The schemes preferred for the motet are *trocheus* (trochaic), *iambus* (iambic) and *dactylus* (dactylic)—and whichever one is chosen by the composer is maintained without alteration throughout the piece. The possibilities of such restrictive procedures being exhausted—procedures which in any case give the composition a tiresome stiffness—from about the year 1250 composers made new efforts in a search for new devices. The *triplum* was the first voice to step out of line, with the breaking up of its long notes into others of shorter duration. Two composers contributed to this liberalizing process, Franco of Cologne and Petrus de Cruce. At the same time another event gave impetus to the rhythmic evolution of the motet, namely the substitution for the metrical Latin texts, used up to this time, for others written in prose.

The latter were better fitted than the former for freeing themselves from the rhythmic modes, since there was a definite
connection between the metric texts and the rhythmic modes.

To sum up—at the end of the thirteenth century the motet
displayed these characteristics: it consisted of at least three
voices, each having its own rhythm and text; Latin was frequently replaced by the vernacular; the tenor was no longer
sought in the liturgical repertory but in popular song, these last
two factors bringing the motet to a flowering unprecedented in
the history of musical forms.

Finally, it must be pointed out that the voices above the *tenor*
were not always written by the same composer, but added later
by others, so that during these centuries the same motet may
appear in two voices in one manuscript, and in three voices in
those of a later date.

*   *   *   *   *

The 'ars nova' proclaimed by Phillipe de Vitry in his treatise of
that name brought about innovations of far-reaching significance: it introduced binary rhythm, chromatic semitones, the
harmonic use of thirds and sixths—as against the intervals
of fifth and octave used exclusively up to this time—this use of
imperfect consonances producing a fuller-sounding type of
harmony.

The motet of the 'ars nova' consisted of three voices—the
tenor or *cantus firmus, motetus* and *triplum,* to which is sometimes
added a fourth, *contratenor,* which was frequently the lowest part.

When the motet of the earlier period and that of the fourteenth century are compared, it can be realized that the latter
already has a definite musical form while that of the 'ars
antiqua' is, in comparison, quite shapeless. The formal basis
of the motet of this new phase was the *tenor,* which was repeated
several times with a more or less identical rhythmic structure,
while the melody changes with each new section or phrase.
This brought about a symmetrical organization of the composition from which was derived a clear-cut musical form. Because
of the rhythmical division of the tenor into symmetrical seg-
ments the motet of the 'ars nova' was called 'isorhythmic'.
The repetition of the successive periods of the *tenor* was sometimes modified by augmentation or diminution, this giving rise

to the contrapuntal devices practised later by the composers of the Netherlands schools.

The motet underwent a new important transformation in this century. While up to this time, the *tenor*, that is the lowest part, was the principal voice, there came into vogue later a new type of motet in which the top part was accompanied by lower instrumental parts. Johannes de Ciconia was probably the author of this innovation—he accompanied his motets with a trumpet. This composer who was responsible, in Italy, for the substitution of the highest men's voices by unbroken voices, brought to the motet form another element of construction of far-reaching importance—imitation.

Dunstable marks a new phase in the history of the motet. He introduced the simplification of the instrumental parts so that they could be performed by voices, and the use of one text by all voices. These innovations were developed further in the work of Guillaume Dufay (*d.* 1474), who made frequent use of canon, and in particular contributed more than any other composer to perfecting the technique of *fauxbourdon*.

Finally, at the end of the fifteenth century appeared the man with whom began the extraordinary flowering of the motet in the sixteenth century, Josquin des Prés (1450–1521). With this composer the abuse of the riddle canon began to disappear, and with it the melodic rigidity of the *tenor*; he freed himself from the domination of the mechanical and formalistic aspects of technique, achieving in his compositions an admirable unity; and with the simplification of technique the text acquired a clarity of enunciation not previously achieved. Over and above all this he brought about a rapprochement between text and music which enhanced its meaning, this heralding the great expressive achievement of the sixteenth-century polyphonists.

In the sixteenth century the word 'motet' had a very wide range of meaning. All liturgical pieces except the mass came under this heading. Various editions of Victoria headed with these words—*Motecta qve partim qvaternis, partim qvinis ... vocibus concinuntur*—contain hymns, psalms, litanies, sequences, antiphons to the Virgin. Actually, going by the titles of many editions the word 'motet' must have been a popular rather than the technical or specific term, this being *cantio*. Thus *Sacrae cantiones, vulgo moteta nuncupata ...* is frequently seen.

The text of the motet is normally derived from the liturgy. Nevertheless many composers have been inspired by the Bible, by early Christian literature and even by secular sources, since the sixteenth-century motet is not exclusively sacred in character. Palestrina, for example, composed a book of motets on the Song of Songs, while in the *Magnum Opus* of Lassus can be found various secular motets composed to extol the virtues of some prince or cardinal, or even to celebrate a wedding, in praise of music, wine and on other secular themes.

(b) The formal structure of the polyphonic motet

The principle of motet construction is bound up with the division of the text into phrases, so that the motet as a whole is made up of musical episodes or sections, each having its own theme. The number of these episodes is determined by the number of phrases in the text, each new phrase giving rise to a new theme, which is stated in imitative or in homophonic style. These two procedures play in continuous opposition throughout the piece, providing admirable contrast, variety and balance.

With this formal structure of the motet there co-exist other principles of construction, such as *cantus firmus* and *canon*. Thus in the piece *Ave Virgo* (1) Guerrero combines motet procedure with canonic imitation, and Victoria, in his motet *Ecce sacerdos* (2) reverts to the idea of *cantus firmus*. Because of this some authors describe these pieces as *motete cantus firmus, motete canonico.* . . .

The division of the motet into different sections does not impair the unity essential to every work of art. The sections are not disconnected fragments juxtaposed—on the contrary, there is between them a close bond and relationship achieved in accordance with the principles set out in the preceding chapter. The overall unity of the piece is safeguarded by the single tonality prevailing from beginning to end. This is never endangered by passing modulations; the intermediate cadences —not final but provisional—by their very nature require something to follow them; and finally, the extended concluding passage confirms completely the feeling of unity attained by the methods listed above.

As an illustration of the foregoing discussion a short analysis is given of the motet *Canite tuba in Sion* by Guerrero. (3)

From the point of view of mode, this belongs to the authentic form of the Dorian mode transposed, with a key-signature of one flat and G as final, the *tenor* part lying within the octave G–G, or final–final. There are cadences on the fourth degree in bars 10, 14 and 29–30; on the fifth degree in bars 17, 22 and 56; and by movement downwards from the sixth onto the fifth degree in bars 32–33 and 48–49.

es Do - mi - ni.

Do - mi - ni, di - es Do - mi - ni.   Ec - ce ve -

ni, di - es Domi - ni. Ec - ce ve - nit, ec -

di - es Domi - ni.

Ec - ce ve - nit,   ec -

ec - ce ve - nit

nit,   ce ve - nit, ec - ce

Ec - ce ve - nit,   ec - ce

ce ve - nit   ad sal - van - dum

ad sal - van - dum nos, ad sal - van - dum

ve - nit, ec - ce ve - nit   ad sal -

ve - nit   ad sal - van - dum nos, sal -

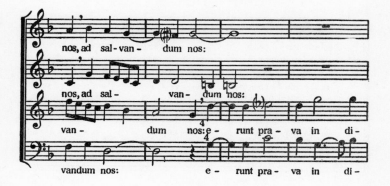

The text is divided into the following phrases

1. *Canite tuba in sion,*
2. (a) *quia prope est* (b) *dies Domini,*
3. (a) *ecce venit* (b) *ad salvandum nos:*
4. *erunt prava in directa,*
5. *et aspera in vias planas:*
6. (a) *veni Domine,* (b) *et noli tardare.*

Phrases 2, 3 and 6 comprise two entries, shown by (a) and (b) in parentheses.

The manner of statement of each phrase is as follows:

1. Imitative polyphony.
2. (a) Homophony, (b) imitation.
3. (a) The two upper voices state a theme in imitation; in their turn the lower voices give out another, different theme which serves at the same time as harmonic support for the first, (b) Imitative polyphony.
4. The lower voices have note-against-note counterpoint which is repeated by the upper voices a fifth higher with the *tenor* completing the harmony.
5. Homophony.
6. (a) Imitative polyphony, (b) Homophony, or what might be called free polyphony.

(c) Motets in two parts

When the text is rather long it is generally divided into two parts, each one becoming a motet. The two parts are generally headed, both in printed editions and manuscripts, with the words *prima pars* and *secunda pars*, the first of these headings often being omitted but the second very seldom.

Sometimes the only connection between the two parts is the mode, this being the case in *Domine non sum dignus* by Victoria; at other times, as against this, the concluding portion of the second part is identical with that of the first.

Thus *Rorate caeli desuper*, (4) the second part of *Canite tuba in Sion*, concludes with the same phrase as the first, *Veni Domine, et noli tardare.*

Generally speaking, the text of motets divided into two parts is taken from some responsory, in which case the main portion of the responsory together with the refrain forms the first part of the motet, the verse, followed without any loss of continuity by the refrain, making up the second.

The antiphons to the Virgin, *Alma Redemptoris Mater*, *Ave Regina caelorum*, *Regina caeli laetare* and *Salve Regina* are also generally divided into two parts.

THE MASS

The composition of the mass in the classical period of polyphony followed the same principles of construction as the motet.

The themes are sometimes personally composed, while others are taken from the Gregorian, popular or polyphonic repertories. In the second case the mass is described as a *cantus firmus* mass, a *chanson* mass or a *parody* mass, these terms referring to the different ways the quoted themes are treated by the composers, as shown in Chap. 13.

All the pieces comprising the mass, *Kyrie*, *Gloria*, *Credo*, *Sanctus*, *Benedictus* and *Agnus Dei* are simply motets of greater or lesser dimensions, whose external form conforms more or less strictly to the following plan:

The *Kyrie* comprises three sections:

(*a*) *Kyrie I*;
(*b*) *Christe*;
(*c*) *Kyrie II*.

The end of each section is indicated by a definite closing cadence, on the final in *Kyrie I*, the dominant in *Christe* and again on the final in *Kyrie II*.

The *Gloria* and to an even greater extent the *Credo*, on account of their length, are usually divided into various sections separated from one another by a perfect cadence, in which all the voices reach a point of repose on a concluding chord of comparatively lengthy duration. The number of sections varies from composer to composer and from one piece to another. Most frequent is the division of the *Gloria* into two parts, the first up to *Qui tollis* and the second from this point to the end.

The division of the *Credo* is less uniform. Up to *Et incarnatus est* usually forms one section; *Et incarnatus est* is generally treated quite independently of the rest of the piece, and with the idea of making this phrase more prominent it is, not infrequently, separated by rests from what precedes and follows it. From

Crucifixus to the end of the *Credo* the number of sections varies from one to three, according to circumstances.

The *Sanctus* constitutes a long sentence, divided up generally in this way:

(*a*) *Sanctus, sanctus, sanctus,*
(*b*) *Dominus Deus Sabaoth*
(*c*) *Pleni sunt caeli terra gloria tua.*
(*d*) *Hosanna in excelsis.*

Hosanna in excelsis is frequently set in ternary rhythm.
The *Benedictus* is usually divided in this way:

(*a*) *Benedictus qui venit*
(*b*) *in nomine Domini.*
(*c*) *Hosanna in excelsis.*

In many masses this *Hosanna* is the same as that of the *Sanctus*. Occasionally the polyphonists compose three settings of the *Agnus Dei*, but almost always they limit themselves to two, the first and third, divided into three phrases:

(*a*) *Agnus Dei,*
(*b*) *qui tollis peccata mundi,*
(*c*) *miserere nobis,* or *dona nobis pacem.*

It will not be superfluous to point out that sometimes some of these phrases are further divided into two, each sub-division having its own theme, one being treated polyphonically and the other in note-against-note counterpoint. This happens more especially with *Pleni sunt caeli et terra | gloria tua. Hosanna | in excelsis,* and *Benedictus | qui venit.*

Within the overall outlines of this plan, to which the polyphonists conformed more or less faithfully, other details can be observed concerning the number of voices employed in different parts of the mass. These can be summed up in the following observations:

(*a*) All the voices sing *Kyries I* and *II,* the complete *Gloria,* the beginning and end of the *Credo, Sanctus, Hosanna* and *Agnus Dei.*

(*b*) A smaller number of voices is used in the *Christe, Crucifixus* and *Benedictus.*

(*c*) In masses for four voices the second *Agnus Dei* is usually written for five, six or more voices, providing an opportunity for the writing of a *canon*.

In conclusion, one should mention the different ways in which the polyphonic composers deal with the different parts of the mass, with the *Kyrie, Sanctus, Benedictus* and *Agnus Dei* on the one hand, and the *Gloria* and *Credo* on the other. While the former are decked in elegant, luxuriant counterpoint, the *Gloria* and *Credo*, because of their length, are composed in a predominantly homophonic style, obviously to avoid prolonging the liturgical action.

THE RESPONSORY

The form of the polyphonic Responsory, as of the Gregorian, is determined by the plan of the Liturgical text. This can be shown clearly by means of the following scheme:

(i) main part of the Responsory;
(ii) refrain;
(iii) verse;
(iv) refrain.

Between the verse and the rest of the Responsory the following stylistic differences are apparent:

(*a*) The principal part of the Responsory is set to a very simple, almost homophonic polyphony, while the verse is in the imitative polyphonic style.

(*b*) As a general rule the verse is set for fewer voices and intended for soloists, while the rest of the Responsory is sung by the whole choir.

THE HYMN

Composers have created the richest collections of polyphony on the hymns of the *divine office*. Among these, that of Palestrina, who composed music for the rites of the religious orders, can be cited as one of the most complete. Victoria also wrote a collection entitled *Hymni totius anni*, published in 1581.

The hymn was generally sung in alteration between the *schola* and the *choir*, the latter singing a strophe in Gregorian chant and the former responding with the next strophe in polyphony. Despite this Palestrina wrote music for all the strophes of various hymns. (5)

Each polyphonic strophe is a little piece in which are wonderfully combined the principle of the motet and that of *cantus firmus*, taken from the appropriate Gregorian melody. This, altered according to the requirements of the composer, provides the motifs from which is woven the imitative polyphonic texture, which makes its appearance, phrase by phrase, in the same order. Normally in the period of classical polyphony the *cantus firmus* is entrusted to the top voice; cases can be found, however, in which it moves from one to another, which led to the term *cantus vagans*, given to it by present-day musicologists. Briefly, each polyphonic strophe of a hymn is a short motet composed on a *cantus firmus*.

If there are several polyphonic strophes, one of the intermediate ones will be set for fewer voices, while in the final strophe the number is often increased, to give an opportunity for the writing of a canon, a procedure by which the polyphonists indicate the conclusion of their works.

PSALMODY

In the study of psalmody two forms must be distinguished: (*a*) simple psalm settings, known as *fabordones*; (*b*) more florid settings.

(*a*) *The fabordón* (6)
This is the simplest form of polyphony. Its musical structure is the same as that of the Gregorian melody, apart from its tonal implications.

Each half-versicle consists of the reciting chord and cadence, the two being clearly separated by the concluding chord of the central cadence.

Here are some brief comments on the various elements that make up the *fabordón*:

1. The intoning of the psalm takes place on a single chord.

2. The central cadence falls, as a general rule, on a chord other than that of the final, the idea being to produce an effect of suspense rather than conclusion.

3. The *fabordón* concludes with a perfect cadence on the

appropriate Gregorian final. This rule admits of exceptions, as for example modes V and VIII, which sometimes finish on C instead of on their respective finals, F and G.

4. Neither intermediate nor final cadences normally extend over more than three bars.

5. The style of the music within these bars may vary from note-against-note counterpoint to the florid style.

This discussion should not be concluded without considering some slight differences which exist between the *falsobordone* of the Roman school and the *fabordón* practised in Spain.

Briefly these differences are that in the *fabordón* the *tenor* is not recited freely but in measured time, with occasional changes of harmony and, what is even more remarkable, ornamented with passing-notes and other contrapuntal devices. (7)

(b) The florid psalm setting
This is the *fabordón* enlarged and extended. In florid psalm settings the recitation or tenor and the separation of the two half-versicles have been dispensed with. The musical structure develops around the appropriate Gregorian melody which forms the *cantus firmus*. The central cadence follows the same procedure as any other passing cadence in polyphony—in it the movement from one half-versicle to the other takes place without any break in the flow of the polyphony. The final cadence observes the same rules as in the *fabordón*. No polyphonic procedure is out of place in this type of psalm setting, where passages in imitative style, in note-against-note counterpoint and in florid style can all be found.

Significant stylistic differences can be observed between psalm settings for four or five voices and those for eight. In the first, used mainly in the *Gospel Canticles*, especially in the *Magnificat*, the polyphony retains its essential and most distinctive characteristics. In contrast to this, in settings for eight voices, the baroque style of the seventeenth and eighteenth centuries can already be seen. The continuity of the melodic line disappears, giving way to a breaking-up of the themes into very short phrases, whose repetitions in alternation between the choirs produce continuous antiphony.

Observations Concerning the
Interpretation of Polyphony

No doubt much disappointment will result from the reading of
this Appendix concerning the interpretation of polyphony.
Many are waiting impatiently for a large-scale treatise crammed
with innumerable detailed rules. This would be very difficult
if not impossible to write, and would be like travelling along a
road in the depth of a dark night without the help of even the
feeblest light.

How was polyphony interpreted in the sixteenth century?
We do not know. All the witnesses of the period, questioned on
this matter, offer no information. Printed editions of polyphony,
manuscripts, writers of treatises, give no assistance. It is a secret
lost for ever, if indeed it ever existed.

Accordingly, all that may be suggested nowadays about the
performance of classical polyphony are ideas arising out of the
study of the music itself, based on today's way of thinking,
which is perhaps not very close to the custom and usage of four
centuries ago. Certainly it is not necessary to be over-anxious
when dealing with a work to be sung in church. The important
thing in this case is that the piece performed should make an
effective contribution to Divine worship, and to the sanctifying
and edifying of the faithful. This can be so even when it is
performed according to contemporary ideas, possibly in direct
contradiction to those of the period in which it was written.

THE MEANING OF THE WORD 'INTERPRETATION'

Nowadays it is synonymous with performance. We set aside any
idea of exegesis, explanation or search for the meaning of a
phrase whose meaning is not obvious. The meaning of sacred
polyphony is always crystal-clear. It is vocal music, written on a
text whose total significance depends chiefly on the meaning

of the words, but also on the exact time appointed by the Church in the mass, Divine office and liturgical cycle: Advent, Christmas, Lent, etc.

And so the meaning of any polyphonic piece whatever cannot be other than that of the text which prompted its composition. Any other view would be an artistic aberration, quite out of keeping with the musicians of the Renaissance, whose genius was nourished in the composition of their immortal works by an ardent and living spirit of extraordinarily vital faith. In addition, it is absurd to rack the brain in search of secret ideas or hidden meanings. There are none. At the most they exist only in the fevered imagination of some choirmaster.

GENERAL PRINCIPLES

1. Above all it is necessary to eliminate any effect that can possibly be traced to a secular origin. It is a principle laid down by His Holiness Pius X in his *Motu proprio*: 'Sacred music must be holy, and accordingly must exclude anything profane, not only in itself, *but in the way in which the singers themselves interpret it.*' (1)

Effects inappropriate to worship are exaggerated vibrato of the voice, portamentos, sobs, forced contrasts and overdone dramatic effects.

The first rule in sacred song [said St. Ambrose] is decorum, reverence (*in canendo, prima disciplina verecundia est*): respect for the place, the congregation, the liturgical function, the sacred text. . . . (2)

2. The liturgy is an infallible guide in musical performance. The liturgy is never expressed extravagantly, in impassioned lyricism nor in heart-rending dramatics.

Liturgical piety is robust in performance, as in its nature. There is no tenderness like that of liturgical piety in its various manifestations; but it is always austere and serene; gentle, but strong. This is so in its text, gestures, rites and symbols; it might be said that clarity and strength of thought regulate the expression of piety, maintaining this within a dignity and gravity which make its gentleness more penetrating and evocative. (3)

The liturgy sets out a well-defined programme to which

each choirmaster should submit, in the assurance that, far from endangering his personality, a weak and feeble thing, it will give it firm support and reveal to him a limitless field of opportunity. Through this the relative will gravitate toward the absolute. (4) Hence the necessity for every choirmaster to have a wide knowledge of the liturgy both historical and, even more important still, doctrinal.

3. The interpretation of classical polyphony must be informed with this idea—that the purpose of sacred music is to glorify God: it is music certainly; but above all it is prayer. Its function is not to fill a vacuum, to amuse or entertain the faithful. On the contrary, it is what gives the greatest effectiveness to the fervent prayer intoned quietly by the clergy, to which they listen in reverent silence. It bears them aloft to contemplation of the mysteries being celebrated in their presence. This is the exalted vocation of which the composers of classical polyphony were fully convinced—a vocation which places a heavy responsibility upon the interpreters of these immortal works. (5)

4. In conclusion, the interpretation should be objective and impersonal, with the objectivity and impersonality appropriate to the liturgy. The choirmaster should not make use of the choir nor of the piece it performs for his own ends, to express his own ideas or to demonstrate his abilities. In such circumstances he would not be a faithful servant of the liturgy, but a slave to his own personality. All dilettantism is out of place in worship. Furthermore, technique and the knowledge of what to do are of value here only in so far as they are subordinated to the liturgy.

EXPRESSION

This word means the art of giving life to the performance of a musical work. There are several aspects to it, the main ones being rhythm, dynamics and colour. Apart from these points, others will be dealt with which, although secondary, should not be overlooked.

TESSITURA

Many polyphonic compositions of the sixteenth century cannot be sung at the pitch at which they are written—they are either too high or too low. Their composers did not write them at a particular pitch because they were sung at that pitch in those days, but because, in their writing, only a few tonalities were acknowledged. How then were they performed? Simply by transposing the piece to a pitch more convenient for the choir. Works written in authentic modes were sung from a tone to a fourth lower, while those written in plagal modes required, though not always, a small shift upwards.

Accordingly the choirmaster must examine the tessitura of the piece he intends to rehearse, especially as it affects the outer voices, and should adjust it to the capacity of his choir, doing his best to find a comfortable range for all the voices, 'without forced shrillness in the high register, or flat intonation, which weakens the choir and produces a grey, murky tone'. (6) If on occasion he finds a composition which, even when transposed, cannot be performed by his choir without gravely endangering its tone, the best advice he can be given is to abandon it and look for something else.

TEMPO

It is quite commonly believed that classical polyphony requires a slow, almost ponderous tempo. Nothing could be further from the truth, nor could anything be more contrary to the spirit which gives life to this art, than those heavy, leaden performances given by nearly every choir. They are the death of polyphony. What then should the tempo be? How is it determined? The witnesses of the period—the theorists—will answer us with a wealth of detail. On the one hand they will equate the duration of a bar with each beat of a human pulse; so that, as a normal man's heart beats at the rate of between seventy and eighty to the minute, it follows that in the sixteenth century they used to sing this number of bars in this space of time, namely between seventy and eighty to the minute. On the other hand, we learn from the same sources that, in Palestrina's time, the semibreve was the standard measurement of the binary bar, (7) which implies that in the space of a minute they used to perform between seventy and eighty semibreves, twice the number of minims, etc. If one of the so-called modern performances is compared with one following the principles just given, the tremendous difference between them will be seen. While, in the second, polyphony regains its true life and natural freshness, in the first it languishes, weak and spiritless, and almost expires. The experiences shared with students in the short course held in Vitoria during the summer of 1954 are recalled. Through force of habit, in the first rehearsals everyone preferred the slow performances, but on the few occasions when the same piece, the motet *Domine non sum dignus* by Victoria, was sung both ways, unanimous preference was declared for the authentic tempo.

This principle should be applied, however, with artistic judgment, not metronomic inflexibility, and there are many other factors which can have a bearing on the tempo of each piece, which the choirmaster should bear in mind. Here are the main ones:

(*a*) *The text*. It is the soul of the piece; the composer has been inspired by it in the first place to compose his musical commentary. Some texts express sentiments of grief, others of sadness, others of wonder; some are festive, happy, triumphal: many contain fervent prayers, some a straightforward narrative. All this has influenced the mind of the composer, who in his turn expresses it in the themes of his composition. These same shades of meaning should suggest to the choirmaster here a quicker tempo, there a slower tempo than usual. It is obvious that an *O vos omnes* requires more moderate movement than an *Exultate justi*.

But different tempos are not only appropriate to different pieces. The content of the text can suggest a change of tempo within the same piece.

(*b*) The rhythmic notation of the phrase also can suggest a slight change of tempo. A florid contrapuntal texture will have a more moderate speed than one composed of long notes. So, for example, in the motet *O magnum mysterium* by Victoria it is appropriate to have an almost imperceptible ritardando in bars seven and eight, to allow for a suitable delivery of the luxuriant melisma adorning the word *sacramentum*. Many choirs obscure this and other most beautiful filigree through not bearing this principle in mind.

(*c*) Homophonic passages can be performed at a quicker tempo, particularly when all the voices move according to the same rhythmic pattern, unless the text expresses grief, lowly reverence or contains a petition. But great care should be taken to avoid sudden changes—the transition from one tempo to another should be gradual, graded through accelerandos and ritardandos, according to circumstances, and carefully judged.

(*d*) The tempo should be held back at the end of the principal divisions of the piece and more especially in the last two or three bars. The exact moment for beginning these ritardandos depends on factors it is impossible to define precisely. It is left to the artistic intuition of the choirmaster to determine this in each particular case.

(*e*) In addition to these internal criteria there are other circumstances which can have an influence in deciding the tempo of a piece; circumstances completely external in character but whose significance should not, on this account, be underestimated. These are the place, and the number of voices. In a very large church it is necessary to sing more slowly than in one that is smaller, this being important because of acoustic conditions. Finally, a small choir can move with greater freedom than a larger one.

COLOUR

Who is unaware of the importance of colour in the performance of a piece of music? Who has not experienced the boredom engendered by hearing a work performed from beginning to end at the same dynamic level, without change of light or contrast of colour? Questions on this topic could be continued indefinitely, in the complete and utter certainty that they would be answered in the same way by all, as it cannot be denied that a musical work performed without colour lacks life.

There are many, on the other hand, who go to the opposite extreme. They consider and act on the principle that a good performance requires a different colour for each note, thus falling into the most ridiculous mannerisms. *In medio virtus*: conductors should avoid performances, which being dead, have no emotional appeal—and they also should steer clear of effect for its own sake. Everything must be subordinated to the requirements of the liturgical text and to art.

(*a*) A good performance should project in space the architecture of the piece, both as a whole and in its more general outlines. Many musical works have a climax—these are the towers of the cathedral, the dome of the basilica, which stand out from the rest of the structure. Everything else must be subservient to this culminating point—the part preceding it rising steadily with the ebb and flow of the waves, little by little increasing in size, despite momentary recession, till the expressive climax, the most telling part of the composition is reached. The part that follows returns by the same route, like an eagle, which after having soared to the heights does not descend vertically, but in gliding movements, in undulating lines, sometimes greater, sometimes smaller in their sweep, until it settles with perfect poise and smoothness. It can happen that the expressive climax may coincide with the end of the work, in which case all that precedes it prepares the way for it—only rarely do we find it at the beginning of a piece.

In many works it is not possible to indicate a point of climax that clearly dominates the whole piece—in such cases it is enough to give each phrase the dynamic expression required by the inner meaning of the text, both actual and implied, aiming over the whole length of the piece for a well-judged proportion and balance. These works are like the smooth movement of sea-waves on a quiet day; none achieves a higher crest than the others; all follow the same design, a line in the shape of an arch with its beginning, its ascent and its descent. The beginning will start sometimes from piano, sometimes from a mezzo-forte level, the ascent will culminate now at a mezzo-forte, now at a forte, the descent reducing to a mezzo-forte, to piano, and pianissimo, depending on what follows it.

The projection of the work should not in any way resemble a blurred picture in which the main idea is obvious enough, but where details are not as clear as they should be. Putting it another way, it is not enough to grade rightly the dynamics preceding and following the point of climax; it is essential also that at these different levels the themes of which they are composed should be given greater or lesser prominence, according to their importance, just as in a photograph of a cathedral. It would not be satisfactory if all that could be seen were the general outlines such as the towers and façades. It is important also to see the cornices, the rose windows, the tympana and other decorative details of the building, for unless these can be seen it loses much of its beauty.

(b) The choirmaster, in studying a piece, should regard as very important the graduation of tone often indicated by the polyphonists in the actual writing of it, especially in pieces for more than four voices. If in a certain passage the composer makes one or two voices rest he obtains *ipso facto* a reduction of intensity, greater or lesser depending on whether the number of voices resting is large or small, without the singers having to make the slightest diminuendo in their singing. If, following the rests, he has all the voices entering at once, the result will be like the sound of the full organ. If, on the contrary, he makes them appear on the scene one after the other, he will produce the effect of a gradual crescendo.

In the same way, effects of light and shade, and contrasts of light, depend frequently on the polyphonic writing. A passage in which the top voice is resting takes on, as a result, something in the nature of a sombre colour, the contrast, or perhaps illumination, being achieved by the opposite procedure when he makes a low voice or voices rest. An excellent example, one of thousands, can be seen in the phrase *et aspera in vias planas* from the motet *Canite tuba in Sion* by Guerrero, appearing twice—the first time for *altus, tenor* and *bassus,* in sombre colours, the second for *cantus, altus* and *tenor,* bright in colour. In this case, as in the earlier example, the choir itself does not have to do a great deal to realize the effects present in the writing—all that is required is a clear articulation at a moderate dynamic level—the rest happens by itself.

(c) The performance of any polyphonic work at all requires a perfect legato. But, of course, legato must not be confused with portamento! Only in exceptional cases, very rarely indeed, should a stabbing or staccato articulation be resorted to. Polyphonic melodies are sisters to the Gregorian melodies—or rather, in many cases, their daughters, and as such they should act in exactly the same way. These agitated and affected airs do not go well with the priestly gravity of liturgical worship. They would be much more suitable for false religious cults, with their convulsive and ridiculous gestures.

For that reason Gregorian chant prefers the curved and undulating line rather than the angular line. The former is gentle;

the latter hard and cutting; the former inspires peace, the latter unrest, and God resides not in unrest, being, and being called the God of peace. (8)

The choirmaster should constantly instil into his singers the principle that classical polyphony is completely alien to our modern conception of the bar, with its strong and weak beats; that the dividing lines have no significance in this art: that they are placed there by editors with the sole purpose of making reading easy.

(d) The choirmaster should devise for himself a method of beating time for the direction of classical polyphony, suited to its nature. As in Gregorian chant, the melodies of the different voices are composed on free rhythm—binary and ternary patterns alternating in a rich amalgam. It goes without saying, that there can be nothing more unsuitable for the interpretation of the polyphonic melodies than the inflexible and angular bar of the present day. Special qualifications should be required from choirmasters: they are appointed much too easily even in seminaries and the major colleges for clergy. In any case, whatever system is adopted by the director he should be given an important piece of advice—to moderate his gestures both inside and outside the church, but especially within it. The choirmaster should comport himself with the same calm and serenity with which the liturgical action unfolds. In this there is nothing violent, nothing unsettling, much less anything absurd or inappropriate. Yet there is a good deal of all of these in the gestures of not a few choirmasters. Why so much restlessness and awkwardness, leaning sideways and forwards, incessant twisting and turning in all directions? All this, ridiculous anywhere, is even more so in the church, where it verges on the irreverent. And the worst aspect of the situation is that none of this is necessary to exercise the most complete control over the singers. The rehearsal room is the place where the choirmaster can use every means at his disposal to obtain his heart's desire in the shape of the best possible performance. In the church, on the other hand, this ought to proceed without being forced along by extravagant methods, almost, it might be said, without any need of a choirmaster at all.

(e) This same moderation is advised in the use of means of expression. It is childish to think that each note should bear a particular colour, that this should be different from that of the preceding or following note. Sixteenth-century polyphony is not a miniaturist art. On the contrary, as in the great pictures of the same period, the same colour fills considerable areas of the canvas. It is necessary to take the greatest care to avoid the unnatural effects of showy over-emphasis. Preoccupation with clarity in performance leads the choirmaster, often unintentionally, to extremes bordering on the grotesque or which may be effective but are out of place. In this connection we recall hearing a choir sing the motet *Innocentes* by Luca Marenzio. Everything was going well, but, on arriving at the words *et dicunt semper*, for no apparent reason the choir broke into an accelerando, with *pizzicatos* and so many other effects on each note, that the whole audience looked at one another instinctively in amazement, an unspoken question in their eyes—What is all this about? In conclusion attention is drawn to the performance of accents, both grammatical and musical. Neither should be attacked with direct hammer-blows in the manner of so many choirs, but in relation to the colouring of the moment.

Where should p, mf, f, ff be used, and when should the colouristic effects be employed? It is extremely difficult to lay down *a priori* definite rules. Each piece is a different picture, whose colouring must be sought and distributed in the spheres of text, music and liturgy. To lay down definite procedures in advance is to put them in danger of being applied indiscriminately to themes of very different meanings. The advice given by Casimiri both to singers and choirmasters in the Foreword of his well-known *Anthologia Polyphonica* is repeated here:

> And so, if the singer wishes to sing wisely, and if the master wishes, in teaching him, to place the greatest emphasis on the most important things, it is essential, first of all, that both should have heard perfect performances of classical polyphony.

Notes

(1) This voice is called *tiple* in some Spanish collections with Castilian text, as for example in the *Villanescas spirituales* of Guerrero. In MS 1372 of the Biblioteca Nacional in Madrid it is called *summum*, a term we have not encountered in any other musical document.

(2) The highest part was performed in the sixteenth century by falsettists or high tenors only when musical establishments did not have boys' voices available. Sometimes they would sing with the unbroken voices, giving them guidance and support. Before the sixteenth century, on the other hand, the highest part was sung by tenors, as all the early polyphonic repertory was conceived in terms of equal voices. Hence the low tessitura sometimes found in the upper parts, very difficult to perform nowadays with boys' voices.

(3) It is not uncommon to find *bassis* for *bassus* in sixteenth-century editions. (See, amongst others, Guerrero's collection of motets published in Venice in 1570.)

(4) If the composition is for equal voices the first and third are on the left-hand page, the others on the right.

(5) The F and C clefs are found occasionally on the fifth line.

(6) These clefs, called *chiavette* or transposing clefs by modern musicologists, were used in order to avoid the use of some sharps and flats in writing. In relation to the four most commonly used—C on the first line, C on the third, C on the fourth and F on the fourth—the transposing clefs raise the pieces a third or a fifth.

(7) There were two types of canon. The first consists of a single melody conceived for singing by different voices, each making its entry at an appropriate distance from the others. Each successive repetition is indicated by the sign of the canon. In the second type the theme is repeated by one or two voices, while others go their own way, their motifs nevertheless quite possibly deriving from the canonic theme. Cf. Zacconi, Luigi. *Prattica di musica.* Venice, 1596, Chap. 56, fol. 44v.

(8) It was possible also to write canons at the distance of second, third, sixth and seventh. But the most common and typical intervals were those mentioned above.

(9) Zacconi. Op. cit., Book 1, Chap. 61, fol. 8or.

(10) In the *Cancionero musical de la Casa de Medinaceli* of Barbieri or the *Cancionero Musical del Palacio*, edited by Anglés (Barcelona, 1947), various examples can be seen. Bermudo writes, in this connection: 'I regard it as perfectly satisfactory as far as the commonly used flats are concerned, that on occasions some voices have them and other voices do not.' *Declaración de instrumentos musicales*. Osuna, 1555, Book V, Chap. 32, fol. 139r.

CHAPTER 2

(1) Santa María, P. Tomás. *Arte de tañer fantasía*. Valladolid, 1565, fol. 8v.

(2) Ibid., fol. 9r. Some Italian authors describe as unsingable notes shorter than the minim, because it was not usual to give these a separate syllable on account of their brief duration.

(3) ... por congregación de términos de aritmética y círculos y semicírculos'. Tovar, Francisco. *Libro de música práctica*. Barcelona, 1510, fol. 33r.

(4) Tapia, Martín de. *Vergel de música*. Burgo de Osma, 1570, fol. 98v. Montanos, Francisco de. *Arte de canto llano y de canto de órgano*. Valladolid, 1592, fol. 9r.

(5) Montanos. Op. cit., fol. 9v.

CHAPTER 3

(1) Tirabassi, Antonio. *La mesure dans la notation proportionelle et sa transcription moderne*. Brussels, 1924; *Grammaire de la notation proportionelle*, Brussels, 1930.

(2) Cf. La transcription en notation moderne du 'Liber missarum' de Pierre de la Rue, in the periodical *Scriptorium*, 1946–7, Vol. I, pp. 119–28; La prolation dans l'edition princeps de la messe 'L'homme armé' de Palestrina et la resolution dans l'edition de 1559; ibid., 1948, Vol. II, pp. 85–102; Le tactus principe generateur de l'interpretation de la musique polyphonique classique; ibid., 1950, Vol. IV, pp. 44–65.

(3) 'Dos maneras diferentes de compás tenemos en la música práctica. En la una manera el compás (como dicho es) se divide y parte en dos partes iguales, y en la otra manera en tres partes también iguales; éste es el compás de la proporción, que por otro nombre llaman ternario, en el cual de tres partes

que tiene las dos se gastan en el golpe que hiere en baxo y una
en el que hiere en alto. . . . Esto se hace cantando dos semibreves o dos mínimas en el golpe que hiere en baxo y una en el
que hiere en alto. . . .' Santa María. Op. cit., fol. 8r.

(4) 'Aunque de las tres partes que tiene el compás ternario o de
proporción, cada parte en sí, respecto la una a la otra es igual,
con todo eso el compás no es igual, sino desigual, siendo el dar
el doble más largo que el alzar; porque se cantan de las tres
las dos partes en el golpe que hiere en baxo y una en alto; así,
un dos en el dar, tres en el alzar; digo que la primera es al dar el
compás y luego con la misma cantidad o tardanza de tiempo
se pronuncia la segunda y al alzar la tercera, como queda
dicho en el sexto libro desde presente tratado' (p. 495, Chap.
XIX). Cerone, Pietro. *El melopeo y maestro.* Naples, 1613, p. 750.

(5) 'El compás en número o proporción ternaria (que otros llaman),
yendo tres figuras en un compás, no se parte en dos partes
iguales como el común binario en dar y alzar, mas la primera
figura es al dar del compás, y luego se pronuncia la segunda y
al alzar la tercera.' Montanos. Op. cit., fol. 14v.

(6) Llorente, Andres. *El porqué de la música.* Alcalá de Henares,
1672, pp. 165, 171, 176, 188 and 120 [190?].

(7) 'Io sarei stato d'animo et di parere scrivendo questa mia
Prattica di Musica di passarme senz'altro alla consideratione
delle figure s'acaso non mi fosse incontrato ch'a fatto a fatto
dissente del parere commune: et tiene che sia un sol semplice
tatto, et questo sia el tatto equale: assegnandomi per ragione
che gl'antichi non usavano nelle loro proportioni altro tatto:
ma che il se sia corrotto a poco a poco per commodità de i cantori,
et non per devere et per raggione; per il che io mi sono immagi-
nato ch'anch'altri si potriano immaginar tal cosa e esser di
simil parere, et che serà bene di ragionar delle sue divisione, et
della forza delle dette divisioni; acciache per il mio dire si
sincere ogni uno, et'ogni uno resti della verità pagato.'
Zacconi. Op. cit., fol. 20v.

CHAPTER 4

(1) Santa María. Op. cit., fol. 9v. Bermudo. *Arte tripharia.* Osuna,
1550, fol. 20v.

(2) 'Hay un tiempo dicho perfecto, el cual se escribe en la forma
siguiente: O. Algunas veces este tiempo tiene una vírgula por
medio y es dicho tiempo perfecto de por medio. En el primero
vale la máxima doce compases, y el longo seis, el breve tres, y el
semibreve uno, dos mínimas en un compás, cuatro semínimas

en un compás, ocho corcheas en un compás y dieciséis semi-corcheas en un compás.' Bermudo. *Arte tripharia,* fol. 19v.

(3) 'Omnis itaque concentus ratio, statim ex signo sibi praeposito colligenda est. Nam illa si ad ternarium, id est, perfectionem pertinebit temporis . . . semibreves singulas, tactibus singulis adaptabimus. Id vero quam facile factu sit, nemo cui haec res aliquando tentata est ignoraverit. Duas minimas hoc modo in tactum redigimus: aut quatuor (ut vocant) seminimas.' Ottomaro, Luscinio Argentino. *De concentus polyphoni ratione commentarius primus.* Strasbourg, 1536, p. 83.

(4) '. . . *sotto l'equale* (tatto) *vanno cantato tutti i canti del tempo perfetto e imperfetto;* e sotto l'inequale tutte le proportioni, e le pro-lationi naturale. *I canti del tempo perfetto* con quelli del tempo imperfetto segnati col semicircolo semplice, *vanno cantati con una semibreve per tatto* servandosi le perfettioni dove vanno; quei canti poi del semicircolo traversato vanno cantati con una breve per tatto'. Zacconi. Op. cit., Book I, Chap. 33, fol. 22r.

(5) Bermudo. *Arte tripharia,* fol. 20v.

(6) Bermudo. Ibid., fol. 22v.

(7) The Perfect is also called Greater and the Imperfect Lesser.

(8) 'La prolación pusieron en la música para duración y extensión de figuras en ella, que esto significa *prolatio, prolationis.* Y así en los tiempos con prolación las figuras tienen mucho más valor que los que no la tienen.' Llorente. Op. cit., p. 152.

(9) 'En estos tiempos con prolación vale la mínima un compás y el semibreve tres, no teniendo número delante.' Ibid., p. 152.

(10) Ibid., pp. 186–7 and 191. Montanos. Op. cit., fol. 8v.

(11) Loc. cit., fol. 51v.

(12) Chapter 30, fol. 108.

(13) 'Si dentro del tiempo, en todas las voces pusieren un puntillo, significa la prolación perfecta y hace al semibreve ser perfecto. Digo en todas las voces, porque a ponerse en una no significaría prolación, sino aumentación. En la prolación valen tres mínimas un compás, y en la aumentación, una.' *Arte tripharia,* fol. 21v.

CHAPTER 5

(1) 'Ars discantus', in Coussemaker, E. *Scriptorum de musica medii aevi nova series,* Paris, 1864–76, Vol. III, p. 60. This definition became so generally accepted that it continued to appear in all musical treatises dealing with this subject.

(2) To anyone wishing to acquire a thorough knowledge of this subject, we advise the reading of Chaps. 36–41 of the work from which we have already quoted frequently—*El porqué de la música*. In few authors is it possible to find so clear and systematic an exposition of this subject, illustrated by numerous examples that make it easy to understand.

(3) 'Si viniere una cifra de tres, es que si dos figuras iban a compás que vayan tres, sean las que fueren, y llámase tripla o proporción sesquialtera. . . .' Tapia. Op. cit., Chap. 42, fol. 96r.

(4) This is the only one used by some polyphonists, e.g. Victoria.

(5) All information given here concerning ligatures is derived from the treatise *In Enchiridion de principiis musicae disciplinae* by Guillermo de Podio, published by Anglés in *Anuario musical* (the journal of the Spanish Institute of Musicology). Barcelona, 1947, Vol. II, pp. 151–73.

(6) There is another way of determining the value of the various notes in ligatures. It is based on comparison of those with the shape of the Gregorian neumes *pes* or *podatus*, and *clivis*. An explanation of the procedure is given in the *Diccionario de la Música Labor*, 1954, Vol. II, pp. 1411–12.

CHAPTER 6

(1) To these eight modes four others were later added: two with their final on A and another two on C. Those having C as their final may be regarded as no more than transpositions of the fifth and sixth modes with a B flat key-signature. Those with their final on A, despite their similarity to the *protus*, contribute a new characteristic. The sixth degree is firmly minor, while that of the first mode is major, or at least variable.

(2) 'dos puntos de licencia, el uno a la parte inferior y el otro a la parte superior'. Santa María. Op. cit., fol. 61r.

(3) Cf. Machabey, A. *Histoire et évolution des formules musicales*. Paris, 1928.

(4) 'el cual de tal manera rige todas las otras voces, que las hace que no salgan de los límites y términos del tono'. Santa María. Op. cit., fol. 63.

(5) See the reference to the use of B flat as a key-signature in modes five and six, on pp. 36–37, above.

CHAPTER 7

(1) This does not indicate indifference to, much less underestimation of foreign theorists. On the contrary, the student

wishing to acquire a real understanding of this subject is advised to read the works of Zarlino, especially his *Istituzioni harmoniche*, and even more important, the Augustinian Steffano Vanneo's *Recanetum de musica aurea*. In Chaps. 14, 36 and 37 of Book III he explains fully, illustrating with examples, all the rules dealing with the *semitonía*.

(2) 'En lo cual . . . gasté dieciséis años continuos de lo mejor de mi vida, pasando innumerables e increibles trabajos de día y de noche, inventando cada día cosas y deshaciendo otras y tornándolas a hacer hasta ponerlas en perfección y en reglas universales, y communicando cosas con personas diestras y entendidas en esta facultad, especialmente con el eminente músico de su majestad, Antonio de Cabezón, temiendo de mí, con el propio parecer y afición, no me engañase en algunas cosas.' Santa María. Op. cit., in the *Prólogo al pío lector*.

CHAPTER 8

(1) 'Es de saber que cláusula es conclusión, o fin, o remate de obra, o de paso, la cual se forma y compone de tres puntos, así como re, ut, re.

'Tres cosas se han de notar en esta cláusula. La primera es que el primer punto ha de ser semibreve, y el segundo, mínima; mas el tercero puede ser cualquiera figura de las ocho.

'La segunda cosa es que el sobredicho semibreve siempre se ha de tomar en alto, al alzar del compás. La tercera cosa es que la mínima que inmediatamente se sigue después del semibreve ha de baxar segunda, y después tornarla a subir, así como fa, mi, fa. Muchas veces acontece que en lugar del semibreve de la cláusula se da mínima con puntillo, y en lugar de la mínima que baxa una segunda, se baxan dos corcheas; pero entonces es glosa, la cual se hace por gracia y galanía.

'Así mesmo la cláusula se hace de dos maneras, la una remisa y la otra sostenida. La remisa se hace siempre con tono, así como mi, re, mi. Y la sostenida con semitono, así como fa, mi, fa.

'De la cláusula sostenida se han de notar dos cosas. La una es que pueden fenescer en cualquiera de las cinco voces naturales, que son ut, re, fa, sol, la, mas nunca en el mi. La otra cosa es que el punto que inmediatamente se baxa después del semibreve, necesariamente ha de ser sostenido, esto es: que en el re, ut, re, el ut, y en el sol, fa, sol, el fa, y en la, sol, la, el sol, necessariamente han de ser puntos sostenidos.

'Así mesmo se ha de notar que hay cláusula corta y cláusula larga; la cláusula corta es la que ya hemos dicho es a saber: la sostenida y la remisa. La cláusula larga se conocerá por estos ejemplos siguientes.' Ibid., Chap. 24, fol. 60 et seq.

(2) 'El primero tono tiene sus cláusulas en desolre (= D) y quinta arriba en alamire (= A). La de desolre es final y la de alamire media, y ambas a dos, sostenidas.

'El segundo tono tiene sus cláusulas en desolre, y en fefaut (= F) grave, y en alamire agudo. La de desolre es final y sostenida. La de fefaut, media y sostenida, y la de alamire, de paso y remisa.

'El tercero tono tiene sus cláusulas en elami (= E) grave, y en gesolreut (= G), y en cesolfaut (= C) agudos. La de elami es final y remisa. La de gesolreut, de pas y sostenida, y la de cesolfaut, media y sostenida.

'El cuarto tono tiene sus cláusulas en elami, y cuarta arriba en alamire; la de elami es final y remisa, y la de, alamire media y sostenida.

'El quinto tono tiene sus cláusulas en fefaut, y quinta arriba en cesolfaut. La de fefaut es final y la de cesolfaut media, y ambas a dos, sostenidas.

'El sexto tono tiene sus cláusulas en fefaut grave, y en alamire, y en cesolfaut agudos; la de fefaut es final y sostenida: la de alamire, media y remisa, y la de cesolfaut, de paso y sostenida.

'El séptimo tono tiene sus cláusulas en gesolreut y quinta arriba en delasolre: la de gesolreut es final y la de delasolre media, y ambas a dos sostenidas.

'El octavo tono tiene sus cláusulas en gesolreut, y cuarta arriba en cesolfaut. La de gesolreut es final, y la de cesolfaut, media, y ambas a dos, sostenidas.' Santa María, Tomás. Ibid.

(3) The notes FEF are used to indicate semitone progression at any pitch. Accordingly Tovar says that the cadence on C in the third mode does not require an accidental because it makes the interval sequence FEF (i.e. a semitone), in this case CBC.

(4) 'El primero y segundo modo traen las cláusulas en su final y diapente (5.ª) encima y diapasón (8.ª) y doquiera que truxeren el fin de las tales consonancias hacen legítima cláusula y no en otra parte: y pues primero y segundo hacen final en re, siempre que harán re, ut, re en las tales partes de las cláusulas, aquel re, ut, re *dista por semitono*; aunque en nombre de voz sea tono, en cantidad es semitono. Así mesmo la, sol, la *distarán*

por semitono. Tercero y cuarto modos vel tenos traen sus cláusulas propiamente en su final que natural es elami; y porque bfami donde es fin de su diapente es dificultoso y muchos veces áspero a las orejas por el diatesaron de fefaut [se refiere al tritono que forman las notas fa–si] es consueto de darles las cláusulas donde trae cada uno de ellos el soeculorum. El cuarto en alamire, así como el primero; mas el primero trae semitono subintelecto en la tal cláusula, como arriba es dicho; y el cuarto trae tono. El tercero modo vel tono trae la cláusula en cesolfaut por la causa susodicha, y diciendo fa, mi, fa, *vide* (3), ya trae el semitono, naturalmente: no es menester acidencia. Así mesmo quinto y sexto modos vel tonos trayendo sus finales en fa y todas sus cláusulas en aquéllos no tienen necesidad de otro alguno adyutorio subintelecto, como primero y segundo modos vel tonos. El septimo y octavo modos traen sus cláusulas en fin de sus consonancias [escalas] como cada cual de los otros antedichos, y tienen necesidad de acidencia en sus cláusulas como el primero y segundo; que así como el primero y segundo modos traen su semitono subintelecto en re, ut, re o la, sol, la así el séptimo y octavo traen semitono subintelecto diciendo sol, fa, sol en gesolreut y en delasolre, donde los tales traen las cláusulas. En estos sobredichos modos en ninguna parte se les debe dar cláusula de asonancia en otro punto si no fuere como dicho es, en las notas finales y diapente encima de aquéllos como cada modo reciben, salvo tercero y cuarto modos vel tonos, que por la causa sobredicha hacen cláusulas en diversas partes, como dicho es.' Tovar. Op. cit., Chap. VII, fol. 34r and 34v.

(5) In his work *Arte de música theórica y practica*, printed in Valladolid in 1592, Montanos approves a cadence on A in the third mode and on G in the fourth. *De Compostura*, fol. 28v–5[9?]r.

(6) 'Muchos componedores . . . y todos en general, curan más de la consonancia que de observar los tales preceptos, pues claramente en todas las composiciones están las cláusulas del primero en sexto, y quinto en cuarto, y así de diversos en diversas; y desta manera podemos decir que no hay sino un modo vel tono de cantar, pues todos son semejantes en las cláusulas como por las tales composiciones parecen.' Tovar. Loc. cit.

(7) 'Aunque es verdad que todas las reglas que hemos puesto, en rigor son verdaderas . . ., con todo vemos que los autores algunas veces no las guardan. Cuanto a las cláusulas, es que algunas veces las cláusulas de un tono se mezclan con las de otro, esto es: que siendo primero se hace cláusula de cuarto en

elami, como lo hace Verdelot en un motete de *Gabriel Arch-angelus*. Y también siendo cuarto se hace cláusula de primero en delasolre, como lo hace Josquín en un motete de *Miserere mei Deus*, lo cual también se hace en todos los otros tonos. . . . Así mesmo, algunas veces en las cláusulas se mezclan los maestros con los discípulos y, por el contrario, siendo disci-pulos, hacen cláusulas de maestros, y otras veces acontece que los componedores, por extrañarse de la música ordinaria, hacen cláusulas que salen fuera del tono, y de aquí viene que hay muchas obras que no tienen tono determinado, y así no se puede conocer de qué tono sean, como se ve en *Si bona suscepimus*, de Verdelot, y en otras muchas obras.' Santa María. Op. cit., Chap. 24, fol. 70v.

(8) . . . en todos los puntos de la frecuéncia de la solfa [escala] de cada tono, pero con dos condiciones. La una es que tiple y la voz más baja nunca fenezcan la cláusula en octava ni en quincena [doble octava], sino solamente en decena [décima]. Pero cualquiera de las otras voces intermedias bien puede acabar con la cláusula en octava del tiple. Esto se entiende cuando la cláusula de paso se hiciera fuera de tono, porque cuando se hiciere en el tono bien puede acabar la cláusula el bajo y el tiple en consonancia perfecta, es a saber: en octava, o en decena [quinta sobre la octava], o en sus compuestas. La otra condición es que después de hecha la cláusula, luego se salga de ella, pues no se hace sino de paso, y así esta tal cláusula más propiamente es solfa que cláusula.' Ibid., fol. 67r.

(9) We find this rule in various authors. Montanos gives it in these words: 'When the interval by which the plainsong rises and falls is a whole-tone, the interval by which the counterpoint falls and rises will be a semitone. This is called the sharpened cadence. When the interval by which the plainsong rises and falls is a semitone, the interval by which the counter-point falls and rises will be a wholetone. This is called the unaltered cadence.' ['Cuando el punto que el canto llano sube y vuelve a bajar son tonos, el punto que baja y vuelve a subir el contrapunto serán semitonos. Esta llaman cláusula sostenida. Cuando el punto que el canto llano sube y vuelve a bajar son semitonos el punto que baja y torna a subir el contra-punto serán tonos. Esta llaman cláusula remisa.' Op. cit., 'Contrapunto', fol. 9r.]

(10) Op. cit., Chap. 24.

(11) 'toda cantilena . . . debe ser adornada de muchas cláusulas y

algunas veces pasos largos le pueden poner. Tanto es más suave el canto cuanto abundare de cláusulas. Tanta fuerza tienen las cláusulas por razón de la perfección que en si contienen que hacen a las disonancias consonar.' *Declaración de instrumentos musicales.* Osuna, 1555. Chap. 29, fol. 136.

(12) 'Las obras comúnmente fenecen en octava (posición melódica entre bajo y tiple) o en quincena (doble octava), *las cuales consonancias siempre han de ser sostenidas. Para lo cual es necesario que las voces intermedias, que son tenor y contralto, o la una de ellas, sean puntos sostenidos.* Los cuales hacen que las consonancias suenen recias y sostenidas,' Santa María. Op. cit., Chap. 24, fol. 89v.

(13) The third and sixth are imperfect consonances.

(14) 'Pues digamos . . . que como podemos comenzar en consonancia imperfecta, podemos acabar con ellas. Mayormente siendo *tercera mayor, la cual tiene gran perfeccion por el uso, que apenas hay clausula de a cuatro voces que la una no quede en decena mayor.*' Op. cit., Chap. 20, fol. 131.

CHAPTER 9

(1) In his *Declaración de instrumentos musicales* published five years later, Bermudo reproduces this chapter almost word for word. (See this work, Chap. 48, fol. 87.)

(2) As has been shown previously, these same rules are given by various non-Spanish theorists. See, among others; Vanneo. *Recanetum de musica aurea.* Rome, 1533, Book III, Chap. 14, fol. 75; Zarlino. *L'Istituzioni harmoniche.* Venice, 1589, Chap. 38, fol. 217. Furthermore, examining the treatises of earlier centuries, we find that these are, if not all quoted by each author, some given by some and some by others.

(3) The Italian theorist Prosdocimus de Beldemandis, in the year 1412, explains an example in his treatise in these terms: 'The sharp . . . in the lower part makes the major third a minor third, with the result that being minor, it is nearer its destination, that is, to the unison immediately following, than when it was major.' [Bequadrum . . . in cantu inferiori positum facit illam tertiam majorem, esse minorem, eo quod in sua minoritate minus distat a loco ad quem accedere intendit, scilicet, ab unisono immediate sequenti quam in majoritate . . .' *Tractatus de contrapuncto,* Coussemaker, III, pp. 198–9.]

(4) 'Whenever an imperfect third (i.e. a lesser third), is followed immediately by a fifth or any other perfect interval, with ascending stepwise movement, that imperfect third should be made perfect with a sharp, being changed into a major third.'

['Quandocumque tertia imperfecta, id est non plena de tonis, immediate post se habet quintam, sive aliam quacumque speciem perfectam ascendendo solam notulam, illa tertia imperfecta debet perfici b duro.'] Johannes de Muris. *Ars discantus*, Coussemaker, III, pp. 68 et seq. An example shows the third E–G sharp followed by the fifth, D–A.

(5) 'The sharp in the upper part makes that minor sixth major, as a result of which, being major, it is nearer to its destination, that is, to the octave immediately following, than when it was minor.' ['Bequadrum in cantu superiori positum facit illam sextam minorem esse majorem, eo quod in majoritate minus distat a loco ad quem accedere intendit, scilicet ab octava majori immediate sequenti, quam in sua minoritate.' Beldemandis. Loc. cit.] 'Whenever an imperfect, that is, a lesser sixth is followed immediately by an octave or any other perfect interval, the upper part ascending by step, it should be made perfect by being changed into a major sixth.' ['Quandocumque aliqua sexta imperfecta, id est non plena de tonis immediate habet post se aliquam octavam sive quacumque aliam perfectam speciem, ascendendo solam notulam, illa tunc duplex(?) sexta imperfecta debet perfici b duro.' Johannes de Muris. Loc. cit.] He cites as an example the sixth E–C preceding the octave D–D. See also Nicholas of Capua in his *Compendium musicale*, written in 1415, published in Paris in 1853 by Justus Adrianus de la Fage, p. 32.

(6) This close proximity of the imperfect intervals—thirds and sixths—to the perfect intervals—unisons, fifths and octaves—is the reason given by all the writers of treatises to justify semitone alteration by use of the sharp or flat, that is, it is one of the explanations for the use of the implied or understood semitone. Its formulation can be foreseen in the texts quoted by Beldemandis: 'minus distat a loco quem accedere intendit'. In 1533 it is found expressed clearly by G. M. Lanfranco in his treatise *Scintille di musica*, published in Brescia in that year: 'The seventh rule is that if you wish to move from an imperfect to a perfect consonance you move from the one nearest to it. . . . So in moving from the third to the unison you use the minor third, and with the octave, the major sixth: and so on.' ['La settima (regola) e che volendo andare da una consonanza imperfetta ad una perfetta, che si vada alla piu prossima: . . . come passando dalla terza all'unisono si gli va con la terza minor: et all'ottava con la sesta maggiore: et simili.' Part IV: Regole delle consonanze per lo contrapunto, p. 115.]

(7) With the expressions 'que forma fa' and 'que forma mi', the theorists indicate the effect of lowering a note a semitone by means of a flat, and of raising it a semitone by means of a sharp, respectively.

(8) 'Todas las veces que yo hubiere de dar unisonus, o alguna de sus compuestas [octavas], viniendo de tercera, o alguna de sus compuestas [décimas], no verné de tercera mayor, que es perfecta, sino de la [tercera] menor, que se dice imperfecta. Más cercana está la tercera menor de unísonus que la [tercera] mayor. Luego si en el canto estuviere puntada una tercera mayor, viniendo a unísonus, no lo haré cantando o tañendo. Comúnmente, cuando viene esta tercera mayor, y ha de ser menor, se remedia en la voz baxa poniendo el tal punto [nota] en la tecla negra que está arriba del signo donde está puntado [escrito]. Este mesmo juicio sea habido viniendo a octava de decena, y a quincena de dieciseptena. Si hiciere una quinta, y viniere a ella de tercera, será de la [tercera] mayor, que es dicha perfecta. Esta tercera mayor es más cercana a la quinta que la tercera menor. Si en lo puntado estuviere la sobredicha tercera mayor (como desde Ffaut hasta alamire [fa–la] viniendo a elami, y al mi de bfami) [mi–si], guardarse ha según que estuviere puntado. Si la tercera fuere menor, remediarse ha en la voz superior, subiendo a la tecla negra más cercana de donde está puntado. Si en esta tecla hubiere algún impedimento por alguna octava, remediarse ha en la voz baja con tecla negra que forma fa. *vide* (7) Comúnmente se guarda esta regla, de la tercera mayor cuando de tercera venimos a formar octava.

'Si de quinta salimos a sexta, para volver a la misma quinta, haremos la sexta menor (que es imperfecta), porque es más cercana de la quinta. Si la voz superior hiciere el movimiento de la sexta y en lo puntado no viniere la sexta menor, hacerse ha con una tecla negra, lo cual será fa [bemol]. Si la voz superior hiciere el movimiento de la sexta, y en el ut no hubiere la sexta menor, hacerse ha con una tecla negra, la cual es fa. Si la voz inferior hiciere el movimiento de la sexta, si en teclas blancas hubiera la sexta menor, aquélla se hará, y si no la tuviere el canto, ha de hacerse con una tecla negra, que es mi [sostenido], la cual está arriba del signo donde está puntado.

'Todas las veces que hiciéremos octava (ahora sea en la cláusula o de huida [de paso] viniendo desde la sexta, será hecha con sexta mayor (que es dicha perfecta), la cual está más cercana de la octava que la sexta menor. Si en lo puntado estuviere, no hay dificultad en hacerla. Hágase como está puntada. Si en lo puntado no estuviere, remediarse ha en la voz superior con tecla negra, que es mi [sostenido]. Si desta manera no se pudiese remediar por causa particular, remediarse ha en la voz baxa con una tecla negra, que será fa [bemol]. En tal caso haciendo cláusula séra de cuarto modo, concluyendo en la voz baxa con semitono y en la alta con tono. . . .

'Lo que en estas consonancias simples he practicado, se guarde en las compuestas. Unísonus se dió con tercera menor, la octava será con decena menor, y así de todas las compuestas. Como la octava es compuesta de unísonos, así la docena de la quinta.

'La sobredicha regla infaliblemente se guarde, excepto si por guardarla viene fa [bemol] contra mi [sostenido] en consonancia perfecta. Consonancia perfecta llamo quinta, octava y todas sus compuestas. Pues en tal caso no se guardará la sobredicha regla, sino el punto se porná en el mesmo signo que esta puntado. Ejemplo de la regla y de la excepción.' Bermudo. *Arte tripharia.* Osuna, 1550, Chap. 38, fol. 33 et seq.

(9) Cf. Zarlino: *L'istituzioni harmoniche*, Chap. 38, fol. 217. On the other hand, the Augustinian theorist Vanneo asserts: 'If by any chance a third preceding a fifth should be minor, the assistance of the sharp should be employed as above to make it major.' ['Si forte tertia quintam praecedens fuerit minor, utendum erit auxilio diesis ut supra, quo fiet major.'] *Recanetum de musica aurea*, Book 3, Chap. 14, fol. 75. In support of this he gives a two-part example—one part moving EDC sharp D, and the other CBAG.

(10) In connection with the three progressions DCD, GFG and AGA, Johannes de Muris writes: 'Whenever the notes AGA occur in plain melodic succession the G should be sharpened and sung like FEF. Whenever GFG occur in plain melodic succession the F should be sharpened and sung like FEF. Whenever DCD occur in plain melodic succession the C should be sharpened and sung like FEF. And it should be noted that in counterpoint no other notes are sharpened but those three, namely G, F and C.' ['Quandocumque in simplice cantu est la, sol, la, hoc sol debet sustineri et cantari sicut fa, mi, fa. Quandocumque habetur in simplici cantu sol, fa, sol, hoc fa sustineri debet et cantari sicut fa, mi, fa. Quandocumque habetur in simplici cantu re, ut, re, hoc ut sustineri debet et cantari sicut fa, mi, fa. Et est notandum quod in contrapunctum nulle alie note sustinentur, nisi iste tres, scilicet: sol,

fa, et ut.' *Vide* Coussemaker, III, pp. 72–3.] The same procedure is suggested by Santa María: 'Similarly when any voice
proceeds DCD, GFG, or AGA, in most cases the C, F and G
are sharpened both in natural and in transposed modes. The
explanation and reason for this is smoothness of progression,
and also because they look like cadences, which are always
sharpened, with the exception of EDE, a cadence which is
left unaltered.' ['Asimismo cuando alguna voz hiciere re, ut,
re, o sol, fa, sol, o la, sol, la por la mayor parte el ut, y el fa, y
el sol son puntos sostenidos así en el lo natural como en lo
accidental [transportado]. La razón y causa desto es por la
gracia de la solfa y también porque parecen cláusulas, las
cuales siempre son sostenidas, excepto haciendo mi, re, mi, que
es cláusula remisa.' Op. cit., fol. 74v.]

CHAPTER 10

(1) The theorists of the sixteenth century and their predecessors
used to call the semitone coming between two notes of the
same name (for example, C–C sharp) the unsingable semitone,
and that found between two notes of different names the singable semitone. Music using the unsingable semitone was
described as chromatic, that using the singable as diatonic,
and that using both intervals as mixed. In view of this,
Bermudo's phrase 'In Spain it has not been used' must refer
only to the non-use of the chromatic semitone in diatonic
music.

(2) 'Tres maneras hallo de segundas en la composición de canto
de órgano, y puesta cada una en su lugar es consonancia. . . .
La tercera manera de segunda es de semitono mayor. El
modo de usarlo (no por vía de consonancia, sino por movimiento melódico de una voz como se usó en el género cromático)
es remozado, y en España no se ha usado, no lo he visto
formalmente escrito, aunque me consta haberse usado, como
dije, en el género cromático, *vide* (1). Siendo bien preparado,
podemos usar del sobredicho tono mayor, según en el ejemplo
siguiente puede ser visto.

. . . . .

'Quien con atención mirare el ejemplo sobredicho hallará
que tres veces damos este semitono que dicen incantable.
Para saber cómo este semitono se preparó y cómo se puede dar
todas las veces que quisiéramos, se noten tres cosas. La primera
que no se dice semitono incantable, porque no se pueda cantar
en toda la anchura de la música, sino se dice incantable en el

género diatónico. Pues como lo que ahora se tañe y canta en composición sea mixto del género diatónico y cromático, hay lugar de hacer el tal semitono mayor. Presupongo lo segundo, que viniendo a una octava de sexta, será con sexta mayor, y no menor, si no hay algún impedimento. Digo lo tercero, que quinta de cuatro tonos no se puede dar, mayormente en la que ha de ser buena. Presupuestas estas tres cosas, el ejemplo es manifiesto. La primera mínima del tenor, puesta en csolfaut [do] había de ser sustentada, y porque el contrabajo da otra mínima [negra] en Ffaut [fa] en quinta, no se puede sustentar, que sería en una quinta dar cuatro tonos. La tercera mínima del tenor puesta en dlasolre[re], forma octava con el semibreve de contrabajo en desolre [re] puesto, y viene desde sexta, que es desde Elami [mi], a csolfaut [do], la cual ha de ser mayor. Luego la segunda mínima del tenor, puesta en csolfaut [do], se porná en tecla negra [sostenido]. Pues poniendo la primera mínima en tecla blanca y la segunda en negra, se tañe el semitono mayor. Y por este artificio se tañe (y aun es cantado de algunos sin que lo entiendan) en la segunda minima del contralto en Ffaut [fa] agudo, y en la segunda del tiple en csolfa [do]. Pues siendo puntados unos mesmos puntos en un signo (por diversas causas), el uno se pone en tecla blanca y el otro en negra. No se escandalizará de lo sobredicho el que supiere qué es música cromática.' Book V, Chap. 32, fol. 138.

(3)   'Esta misma distancia de un tono y dos semitonos menores usan algunos tañedores en sola una voz de salto (aunque con escrúpulo y temor), porque les parece ser contra arte aprobada hacer movimiento de cuarta y no tener dos tonos y un semitono. Para quietar a los tales y enseñar a los principiantes digo poderse hacer, y si es contra arte diatónica, no lo es contra arte semicromática que es la música que al presente usamos. Y porque mejor se entienda miren el ejemplo siguiente:

·   ·   ·   ·   ·

'El contralto y el tiple hacen la dicha cuarta, y se hizo porque el contralto acometió cláusula con el contrabajo y se la tomó el tenor, y el tiple acometió cláusula con el tenor y se la tomó el contralto. . . . No hay consonancia más usada que esta cuarta yendo el canto gradatim o seguido, y se hace todas las veces que en una cuarta sustentamos el punto inferior. . . . Ya que tanto es en uso gradatim, no veo inconveniente porque no se use de salto, mayormente siende preparado con cláusula disimulada, como aparece en el ejemplo superior. Pongo por regla cierta, aquel movimiento poderlo hacer una voz de canto de órgano de un golpe (mayormente en el órgano, donde se puede ciertamente formar) que se hizo gradatim, siendo preparados.' Ibid.

(4) '... tened por infalible la regla que siendo el tal movimiento preparado y no teniendo impedimento se pueden todos muy bien dar y es conforme al arte semi-cromático que es la música que en estos tiempos se tañe y en composición se canta.' Ibid.

CHAPTER II

(1) We do not wish to imply that any underlaying of text which does not produce discrepancies among the singers is necessarily satisfactory. It is, of course, well known that the beauty and sonority of a work may vary considerably depending on how this is done. And above all, it should not be forgotten that when the composer is a true artist the text is the life and soul of the composition.

(2) Cf. Anglés, H. *La música en la Corte de los Reyes Católicos.* Madrid, 1941, p. 138.

(3) Only in Montanos can be found this note: 'The setting of text to music should be in longer note-values, so that it may be better understood—not in crotchets except where this is necessary.' (*Arte de música,* in the treatise on *Canto de órgano,* fol. 7v.)

(4) Zarlino, Gioseffo. *L'Istituzioni harmoniche.* Venice, 1573; Vicentino, Nicolas. *L'antica musica ridotta alla moderna pratica.* Rome, 1555; Vanneo, Steffano, O.S.A. *Recanetum de musica aurea.* Rome, 1533.

(5) 'La prima regola adunque sarà di porre sempre sotto la sillaba longa o breue una figura conveniente, di maniera che non si odi alcuno barbarismo: porchioche nel canto figurato ogni figura cantabile che sia distinta et non legata (da la seminima et tutte quelle che sono di lei minori in fuori) porta seco la sua sillaba. . . .

La seconda regola è, che ad ogni legatura di più figure o note sia posta nel canto figurato o nel piano non se le accommoda più di una sillaba nel principio.

La terza che al punto il qual si pone vicino alle figure nel canto figurato, ancora che sia cantabile, non se gli accommoda sillaba alcuna.

La quarta che rare volte si costuma di porre la sillaba spora alcuna seminima, ne sopra quelle figure che sono minore di lei; ne alla figura che la segue immediatamente.

La quinta che alle figure che seguono immediatamente li punti della semibreve et de la minima, le quali non siano di tanto valore quanto sono tali punti, si como la seminima dopo il punto della semibreue et la chroma dopo il punto della minima, non si costuma di accompagnarle alguna sillaba, et cosi à quelle che seguono immediatamente tali figure.

La sesta quando si porra la sillaba sopra la seminima, essendo bisogno, si potrà anco porre un'altra sillaba sopra la figura seguente.

La settima che qualunque figura, sia qual si voglia, che sia posta nel principio della cantilena, o sia nel mezo dopo alcuna pausa, di necessità porta seco la pronuntia di una sillaba.

La ottava che nel canto piano non si replica mai parola o sillaba, ancora che si odino alle volte alcuni che lo fanno, cosa veramente ma nel figurato tali repliche si comportano; non dico gia di una sillaba, ne di una parola, ma di alcuna parte della oratione quando il sentimento è perfetto; et ciò si può fare quando vi sono figure in tanta quantità che si possono replicare commodamente, ancora che il replicare tante siate una cosa (secondo'l mio giudicio) non stia troppo bene se non fuse fatto per isprimere maggiormente le parole, che hanno in se qualche grave sentenza, et fusse degna di consideratione.

La nona che dopo l'havere accommodato tutte le sillabe che si trovano in un periodo o vere in una parte della oratione alle figure cantabili, quando resterà solamente la penultima sillaba et l'ultima tale penultima potrà havere alquante delle figure minori sotto di se, como sono due, o tre, et altra quantità, pur che la detta penultima sillaba sia longa et non breve, perciòche se fusse breve si verrebbe à commetere il barbarismo, il perche cantando in tal modo si viene à far quello che molti chiamano la neuma, che si fa quando sotto una sillaba si proferisce molte figure; ancora che essendo poste cotali figure in tal maniera si faccia contra la prima regola data.

La decima et ultima regola è che si la sillaba ultima della oratione dè terminare, secondo la osservanza delle date regole, nella figura ultima della cantinela.' *L'istituzioni harmoniche.* Venice, 1573, p. 421.

(6) According to the Italian authors singable notes were those of greater value than the crotchet.

(7) 'Animadvertendum est etiam ab optimo compositori longam prolationis syllabam semibrevi notulae, ac brevem minimae adherere constituat, seu aliter: minimae longam, brevemque

seminimae accommodet ut notulae cum verbis una coniunctae barbaricos evitent modos. Saepe enim nonnulli solent eorum cantilenis ineptissimae breves syllabas semibrevibus notulis ac longas minimas. . . .' *Recanetum de musica*, fol. 93v.

(8) ' . . . When a composition has more notes than syllables and it is necessary for a vowel to be spread over several notes, you must observe this rule: When a vowel extends over crotchets and quavers you must not pronounce the next syllable above the first white note immediately following the black note, but on the second white note following the black note.' ['. . . Quando la compositione haura più note che sillabe, e che sia necessario con una vocale correre con più note, quest'ordine si terrà, che quando si correrà con una vocale sopra le seminime è sopra le crome che non si proferisca la sillaba sopra la prima bianco doppo la nera subito, ma doppo la nera sopra la seconda bianca. . . .' *L'antica musica ridotta alla moderna pratica* fol. 86v.]

(9) ' . . . and whenever a composer in a composition makes the singer repeat a noun when this is not necessary, (because) that repetition says nothing.' ['. . . E qualche volta il compositore nella compositione farà ch'il dirà due uolte un nome que non si deue, (perche) quella replica non uuol dir niente. . . .' Ibid., loc. cit.]

(10) Ibid., loc. cit.

CHAPTER 12

(1) See bars 21 and 56 of the motet *O vos omnes* by Victoria, *Opera Omnia*, Vol. I, p. 27. Santa María uses it also in one of the examples given in his *Arte de tañer fantasia*.

(2) Cf. *Suplemento polifónico* de '*Tesoro Sacro-Musical*', No. 29, p. 10, bar 50.

(3) Cf. Rubio, S. *Antología Polifónica Sacra*, vol. I. Madrid, 1954, p. 108. Actually Cardoso's chord is the same as the augmented sixth, but in root position, namely a minor triad with the lowest note raised a semitone. (From here onward *Antología Polifónica Sacra* will be indicated by the abbreviation APS.)

(4) Among the Italians of the Roman School some of the more progressive, for example, Francesco Anerio, use it.

(5) This is one of the reasons on the basis of which Raffaele Casimiri (*Una 'Missa Dominicalis' falsamente attribuita a Tommaso Ludovico de Victoria;* in 'Note d'archivio', Vol. X, No. 3, pp. 185–8) and Hans von May (*Die Kompositionstechnik T. L. Victorias*, Berne and Leipzig, 1943, pp. 143–51), deny Victoria's

authorship of *Missa Dominicalis*, published by Pedrell in Vol. VIII of *Opera Omnia*, pp. 5–14.

(6) The term 'dead interval' is given to those intervals whose notes have no melodic connection, owing to the fact that the first is the conclusion of one phrase or period while the second is the beginning of another.

(7) Morales, for example used it sometimes. See *Opera Omnia*, Vol. II, p. 27, bar 8.

(8) Victoria gives instances of the ascending minor sixth included in the formation of the principal motif of the piece. The responsory *Tenebrae factae sunt* and the motet *Ecce Dominus veniet* may be quoted as examples.

(9) Cf. APS, Vol. I, *Canite tuba in Sion*, p. 1, bar 32; *Rorate caeli desuper*, p. 5, bar 3; *Veni, Domine*, p. 13, bars 9, 20, 27, 40; *Dies sanctificatus*, p. 21, bar 31; *Emendemus in melius*, p. 63, bars 21, 41, 60, and many others not difficult to find.

(10) In the second *Agnus Dei* of his *Missa de Beata Virgine* for five voices, Morales writes an ascending major sixth, C–A, four times. Cf. *Opera Omnia*, Vol. III, Part I, p. 110.

(11) Its use in such circumstances is so frequent that we refrain from quoting examples.

(12) Cf. APS, *Adoramus te, Christe*, Lassus, p. 80, bar 16; *Pueri Hebraeorum vestimenta*, Zorita, p. 98, bars 21 and 65; *Spiritus Sanctus*, Vivanco, p. 248, bar 54; *Veni Creator*, Guerrero, the strophe *Per te sciamus*, p. 258, bar 8; *Pange lingua*, Victoria, the strophe *Genitori*, p. 331, bar 18. Innumerable examples of this sort are found in all composers. But this is not all: at times the interval of the octave occurs between two quavers instead of between a quaver and another longer note. See the *Missa de Beata Virgine*, for five voices, by Morales, *Opera Omnia*, Vol. III, Part I, p. 68, bar 7. The value of the first note of the interval may even be a semiquaver, as can be seen in bar 11 of p. 6 of Vol. I of Morales' *Opera Omnia*.

(13) Cf. APS Vol. I, p. 6, bar 14.

(14) In the golden age of polyphony it is difficult to find the ascending *échappée*; on the other hand it was in common use in the first half of the sixteenth century. In the *Gloria* of the *Missa Hercules*, Josquin des Prés uses it three times within the restricted space of three bars. Other authors give the *échappée* the name of *nota cambiata*.

(15) Cf. APS, *Gloria in excelsis Deo*, Esquivel, Vol. I, p. 27, bar 24, between *altus* and *bassus* there are fifths separated by only a quaver; *O magnum mysterium*, Victoria, p. 34, bar 27 between

cantus and *tenor* are two other perfect fifths separated by two semiquavers. Instances like these are very common.

(16) This occurs principally in pieces for equal voices. The writing is actually correct; nevertheless the effect is of genuine parallel fifths and octaves. It may be seen in innumerable examples which can be cited, as for instance in the connection between the conclusion of bar 31 and the first part of bar 32 in the motet *Duo seraphim* by Victoria. The effect is of two perfect fifths, the first being produced by *bassus* and *tenor II* and the second by *tenor I* which at this point is the lower, and *tenor II*. In bar 14 of *O sacrum convivium* by Viadana the ear hears three octaves and three fifths, though the part writing is perfectly correct.

Viadana: 'O sacrum convivium'

ESCRITURA   EFECTO.

(17) The frequency of false relations in the classics of polyphony is common knowledge. What is remarkable is the shortness of the distance so often separating the notes concerned. Out of many examples that can be quoted, *Magi viderunt stellam* by Victoria, is given (APS, Vol. I, p. 54, bar 72). If the first voice is held back slightly a sudden clash can be produced by hearing the same note sharp and natural simultaneously.

(18) This descending melodic movement of the leading note, regarded by Casimiri as a personal characteristic of Victoria (See *Il Vittoria* in *Note d'archivio*, Vol. XI, No. 2, p. 134), was used also by other composers. Quite often the *échappée* or *cambiata* is no more than a suspended leading note with a descending resolution.

CHAPTER 13

(1) Gevaert, A. *La mélopée antique dans le chant de l'Eglise latine.* Ghent, 1895, p. 123.
(2) Cf. Rubio, S. *XXIV Cantica Sacra in honorem S.P. Agustini.* Bilbao, 1956, p. 6.
(3) Cf. *Opera Omnia*, Vol. II, p. 157.
(4) Ibid., p. 149.
(5) Ibid., p. 192.
(6) Ibid., p. 174.
(7) Ibid., p. 184.

(8) Cf. APS, Vol. I, p. 13.

(9) *Opera Omnia*, Vol. IV, p. 1.

(10) Cf. APS, Vol. II, p. 285.

(11) *Opera Omnia*, Vol. VI, p. 102.

(12) APS, Vol. I, p. 28.

(13) Ibid., p. 49.

(14) Ibid., p. 253.

(15) Ibid., p. 131.

(16) *Opera Omnia*, Vol. I, p. 41.

(17) APS, Vol. II, p. 229.

(18) Fernando de las Infantas, even more than most an admirer of the Gregorian melodies and a stalwart champion of their integrity, made use of them in all his collections of motets, but he also composed a set of contrapuntal exercises on psalm tones which he published in 1579 in Venice under the title *Plura modulationum genera quae vulgo contrapuncta appellantur super excelso gregoriano cantu, omnibus musicam proficientibus utilissima.* In Mitjana's opinion this work occupied in respect of the art of vocal polyphony in the sixteenth century a position analogous to that of Bach's *Well-tempered Clavier* in connection with the composition of fugues. (*Encyclopédie de la musique et Dictionaire du conservatoire*, Vol. VI, p. 1971.)

(19) This work contains invitatorio and psalm 94; antiphons and lessons for the first nocturn; antiphons and first lesson for the second nocturn; antiphons, first lesson and responsory *Libera me Domine de morte aeterna* for the third nocturn: the *Benedictus* from the Laudes and *Requiescant in pace*; *Mass*, without sequence or tract; from the Gradual, *Sicut cervus desiderat*; then from the Benedictus, *Sana me Domine*; and in place of the Communion, *Absolve, Domine animas eorum.* With the exception of the lessons and of another part of the mass, the rest of this work is a most austere polyphonic commentary on the appropriate Greogrian melodies. The Gregorian melody does not move from one voice to another and is presented in notes of long duration. (See the two antiphons published in No. 5 of *Tesoro Sacro-Musical*, 1955, pp. 40–42.)

(20) *Opera Omnia*, Vol. I, p. 1.

(21) Ibid., Vol. II, p. 93.

(22) The two masses were printed in Venice in 1540. Anglés has published one in Vol. I of *Opera Omnia*, pp. 193–237. Among other composers who wrote masses on this song Dufay, Binchois, Compère, Orto, Vacqueras, Josquin des Prés, Palestrina and Carissimi immediately come to mind.

(23) *Opera Omnia.* Vol. II, pp. 38–55.

(24) Ibid., pp. 56–68.

(25) Ibid., pp. 69–80.

(26) Ibid., pp. 145–61.

(27) Ibid., pp. 162–77.

(28) Ibid., Vol. IV, pp. 29–55.

(29) Ibid., pp. 56–71.

(30) *Opera Omnia,* Vol. I, p. 53; APS, Vol. I, p. 231.

(31) APS, Vol. I, p. 5.

(32) *Opera Omnia,* Vol. IX, p. 63; *Repertorium Societatis Polyphonicae Romanae,* ed. Raffaele Casimiri, Vol. I, p. 1.

(33) APS, Vol. I, p. 1.

(34) *Opera Omnia,* Vol. IV, p. 151; *Repertorium S.P.R.,* Vol. I, p. 51.

(35) *Opera Omnia,* Vol. V, p. 172; *Anthologia Polyphonica* (Casimiri), Vol. I, p. 47.

(36) *Opera Omnia,* Vol. I, p. 6; APS, Vol. II, p. 181.

(37) *Opera Omnia,* Vol. I, p. 14; APS, Vol. I, p. 54.

(38) *Suplemento Polifónico* of *Tesoro Sacro-Musical,* No 28, p. 562.

(39) *Repertorium S.P.R.,* motet *Estote fortes in bello,* Vol. IV, p. 15.

(40) *Opera Omnia,* Vol. V, p. 125; *Repertorium S.P.R.,* Vol. III, p. 39.

(41) *Opera Omnia,* Vol. V, p. 140: *Suplemento Polifónico* of *Tesoro Sacro-Musical,* No. 19, p. 400.

(42) Ref. note 32, above.

CHAPTER 14

(1) APS, Vol. I, p. 1.

(2) Ibid., Vol. II, p. 70; see also Palestrina's motet *Surrexit pastor; Opera Omnia,* Vol. V, p. 177; *Anthologia Polyphonica* (ed. Casimiri) Vol. I, p. 50.

(3) APS, Vol. I, p. 67.

(4) Ibid., p. 59.

(5) See note (37), Chap. 13.

(6) APS, Vol. I, p. 1.

(7) The same preference for keeping the entry of the lowest voice till last is maintained by Bach in most of the fugues of his *Well-tempered Clavier,* especially in those for three voices. Cf. Krehl, Stephan. *Fuga.* Colección Labor, Barcelona, 1930, p. 270.

(8) *Opera Omnia,* Vol. XIII, p. 1; *Musica Divina,* Anno I, No. IV. Ratisbon, 1881.

(9) An example of metrical changes may be seen in the words *tuo gremio* of the motet *Sancta et immaculata Virginitas* by Morales, *Opera Omnia,* Vol. II, p. 17.

(10) *Opera Omnia,* Vol. I, p. 11; APS, Vol. I, p. 34.

(11) APS, Vol. I, p. 1.
(12) *Omnia Opera*, Vol. I, p. 40; APS, Vol. I, p. 280.
(13) APS, Vol. II, p. 48.
(14) Ibid., Vol. I, p. 51.
(15) *Opera Omnia*, Vol. II, p. 75; APS, Vol. II, p. 9.
(16) APS, Vol. I, p. 258.
(17) Ibid., Vol. II, p. 107.
(18) *Opera Omnia*, Vol. VI, p. 60; APS, Vol. II, p. 141.
(19) APS, Vol. II, p. 153.
(20) *Opera Omnia*, Vol. II, p. 35.
(21) APS, Vol. I, p. 221.
(22) Ibid., Vol. I, p. 67.
(23) *Repertorium S.P.R.*, Vol. IV, p. 1.
(24) *Opera Omnia*, Vol. II, p. 8; APS, Vol. II, p. 82.

CHAPTER 15
(1) APS, Vol. II, p. 48.
(2) *Opera Omnia*, Vol. I, p. 46.
(3) APS, Vol. I, p. 1.
(4) Ibid., p. 5.
(5) Casimiri, Raffaele: *Il Codice 59 dell'archivio musicale Lateranense, autografo de Giov. Pierluigi da Palestrina*, pp. 74–5, Rome, 1919. In a 37-page appendix Casimiri publishes the strophes not published by Palestrina in the collection of hymns of 1589.
(6) Italian—*falsobordone;* Spanish—*fabordón.* (See p. 128 below.)
(7) Pedrell published a fine collection of *fabordones* in Vol. VI of his *Hispaniae Schola Musica.* Barcelona, 1897.

APPENDIX
(1) *Motu proprio.* I. General principles, 2.
(2) Cardinal Gomá. *El valor educativo de la liturgia católica.* Vol. II, 4th ed. Barcelona, 1954, p. 151.
(3) Ibid., p. 201.
(4) Sanson, J. *Palestrina ou la poésie de l'exactitude.* Paris, 1939, p. 15.
(5) Zehrer, F. *L'interpretazione moderna della Polifonia sacra classica: difetti da evitare*; in 'Atti del Congresso Internazionale di musica Sacra' (held in Rome in 1950). Tournai, 1952, p. 339.
(6) Cf. Rubio, S. *Canciones espirituales polifónicas*, Vol. I. Madrid, 1955; Foreword by Jose Artero, p. iv.
(7) Casimiri, Raffaele. *La polifonia vocale del sec. XVI e la sua trascrizione in figurazione musicale moderna.* Rome, 1942, pp. 11

M

and 15–16; Zehrer. *L'interpretazione della polifonia*, loc. cit., p. 337.

(8) Prado, G. *El canto gregoriano*, Colección Labor. Barcelona, 1945, p. 99.

Bibliography

I. BOOKS, TREATISES, DISSERTATIONS

AARON, P. *I tre libri dell' Instituzioni armonica*. Bologna, 1516.

AARON, P. *Il Toscanello in musica*. Venice, 1523.

AARON, P. *Trattato della natura e cognizione di tutti gli tuoni di canto figurato*. Venice, 1525.

AARON, P. *Lucidario in musica*. Venice, 1545.

ABDY WILLIAMS, C. A. *Story of Notation*. 1903.

ABERT, J. *Die Musikanschauung des Mittelalters und ihre grundlagen*. Leipzig, 1905.

ADLER, G. *Studie zur Geschichte der Harmonie* (on the *fauxbourdon*). Vienna, 1881.

ADLER, G. *Der stil in der Musik*. Leipzig, 1911.

ADLER, G. *Handbuch der Musikgeschichte*. Frankfurt, 1924. (2nd Ed., 1–2, Berlin-Wilmersdorf, 1930.)

ANGLÉS, H. *El codex musical de las Huelgas*, 3 vols. Barcelona, 1931.

APEL, W. *Accidentien und Tonalität in den Musikdenmälern des 15. und 16. Jahrhunderts*. Berlin, 1936.

APEL, W. *The Notation of polyphonic music 900–1600*. 2nd Ed. Cambridge, Massachusetts, 1949.

ARANDA, M. DE *Tractado de canto mensurable y contrapunto*. Lisbon, 1535.

ARTUSI, J. M. *L'arte del contrappunto ridotto in tavole*. Venice, 1586.

AUBREY, P. *Cent motets du xiiie siécle*, 3 vols. Paris, 1908.

BACCUSI, IPPOLITO, O.S.A. *Regulae spirituales melodiae seu Liber spiritualium cantionum*. Antwerp, 1617.

BALMER, L. *Orlando di Lassos Motetten. Eine stilgeschichtliche Studie*. Berne, 1938.

BAÜERLE, H. *Die 7 Busspsalmen Lassos*, 1906. (Doctoral thesis.)

BELLERMANN, H. *Die Mensuralnoten und Taktzeichen des xv. und xvi. Jahrhunderts*. Berlin, 1858. (3rd Ed., revised by J. Wolf, 1930.)

BERMUDO, FR. J. *Arte tripharia*. Osuna, 1550.

BERMUDO, FR. J. *Declaración de instrumentos*. Osuna, 1555.

BESSELER, H. 'Musik des Mittelalters und der Renaissance', in *Handbuch der Musikwissenschaft*, by E. von Bücken. Potsdam, 1931.

BESSELER, H. *Bourdon und Fauxbourdon*. Leipzig, 1950.

BOHN, P. 'Glareani Dodekachordon', German translation in *Gesellschaft für Musikforschung*, Vol. xii. Leipzig, 1889.

BORREN, CH. VAN DEN *Origines et dévelopement de l'art polyphonique vocal du xviémes.* 1920.

BORREN, CH. VAN DEN 'Une "messe-canzonetta" et un "magnificat-chanson" d'Orlando di Lasso', in *Rivista Musicale Italiana*, 1927, pp. 603 et seq.

BORREN, CH. VAN DEN *Orlando di Lasso*. Milan, 1944.

BRAMBACH, W. *Das Tonsystem und die Tonarten des christlichen Abenlandes im Mittelalter.* Leipzig, 1881.

BRENET, M. *Musique et Musiciens de l'ancienne France.* Paris, 1911.

BUKOFZER, M. *Studies in Mediaeval and Renaissance Music.* New York, 1950.

CASELLA, A. *L'evolution de la musique à travers l'histoire de la cadence parfaite.* London, 1924.

CASIMIRI, R. *Il 'codice 59' dell archivio musicale lateranense, autografo di Giov. Pierliugi da Palestrina.* Rome, 1919.

CASIMIRI, R. *La polifonia vocale del sec. xvi. e la sua trascrizione in figurazione musicale moderna* (concerning a review by Antoine Auda). Rome, 1942.

CERONE, D. P. *El melopeo y maestro. Tratado de música theórica y práctica.* Naples, 1613.

CIRUELO (CIRUELUS), P. *Cursus quattuor mathematicarum artium liberalium.* Alcalá, 1526–8.

COUSSEMAKER, E. DE *Scriptorum de musica medii aevi nova series*, 4 vols. Paris, 1864–76.

COUSSEMAKER, E. DE *Histoire de l'harmonie au moyen âge.* Paris, 1852.

COUSSEMAKER, E. DE *L'harmonie au moyen âge*, Paris, 1856.

COUSSEMAKER, E. DE *Les harmonistes des xiie et xiiie siècles.* Paris, 1864.

COUSSEMAKER, E. DE *L'art harmonique aux xiie et xiiie siècles.* Paris, 1865.

DÉCHEVRENS, A. *Composition musicale et composition littéraire.* Paris, 1910.

D'INDY, V. *Cours de composition musicale*, 2nd. Ed., Vol. i, Paris, 1902.

DONI, J. B. *Compendio del trattato de'generi e de'modi della musica.* Rome, 1635.

DUFOURCQ, N. *La musique des origines à nos jours.* (In collaboration). Paris, 1946.

DURÁN, D. M. *Súmula de canto de órgano, contrapunto y composición.* Salamanca (undated).

EISERING, G. *Zur Geschichte des mehrstimmgen Proprium missae bis um 1560*, 1912.

EMANUEL, M. *Histoire de la langue musicale*, 2 vols. Paris, 1911.

FELINI, R. *I classici antichi e la loro esecuzione.* Turin, 1920. (Published in Spanish in the periodical *Musica Sacro-Hispana*, 1914, Nos. 8, 9, 10 and 11.)

FELINI, R. *Il direttore di coro.* Turin, 1920.

FELLERER, K. G. *Der Palestrinastil und seine Bedeutung in der vokalen Kirchenmusik des 18. Jahrhunderts.* Augsburg, 1919.

FELLERER, K. G. *Beitrage zur Musikgeschichte Freisings.* Freising, 1926.

FERNANDEZ, A. *Arte de música de canto dorgam e canto cham.* Lisbon, 1626.

FICKER, R. 'Beiträge zur Chromatik des 14. bis 16. Jahrh.' in *Studien zur Musikwissenschaft*, by Guido Adler, ii, 1914.

FICKER, R. 'Formprobleme der mittelalterlichen Musik', in *Zeitschrift für MW* (1924–5), vii, pp. 195–213.

FOGLIANO (FOLIANUS), L. *Musica theorica.* Venice, 1529.

FROSCH, J. *Rerum musicarum opusculum rarum ac insigne*, Strasbourg, 1535.

GAFORI (GAFURIUS), F. *Practica Musicae.* Milan, 1496.

GAFORI (GAFURIUS), F. *Angelicum ac divinum opus musicae.* Milan, 1508.

GAFORI (GAFURIUS), F. *Practica Musicae.* Venice, 1512.

GASPERINI, G. *Dell'arte d'interpretare la scrittura della musica vocale cinquecento.* Florence, 1902.

GASPERINI, G. *Storia della semiografia musicale*, Milan, 1905.

GENNRICH, F. *Abriss der frankonischen Mensuralnotation.* Nieder-Modau, 1946.

GENNRICH, F. *Abriss der Mensuralnotation des xiv. Jahrhunderts und der ersten Hälfte des xv. Jahrhunderts.* Nieder-Modau, 1948.

GERBERT, M. *Scriptores ecclesiastic de musica*, 3 vols. St. Blasien, 1784. (Facsimile Ed., Milan, 1931.)

GERBERT, M. *De cantu et musica sacra a prima ecclesiae aetate usque ad praesens tempus*, 2 vols. St. Blasien, 1774.

GLAREAN, H. *Dodecachordon.* Basle, 1547.

GRIESBACHER, P. *Kirchenmusikalische Stilistik und Formenlehre*, i–iv, Ratisbon, 1912–16.

GROSSMANN, W. *Die eineitenden Kapital des Speculum Musicae von Johannes de Muris. Ein Beitrag zur Musikanschauung des Mittelalters.* Leipzig, 1924.

HALLER, M. *Trattato della Composizione Musicale Sacra secondo le tradizione della Polifonia classica.* An Italian translation from the German by G. Pagella. Turin, 1926.

HEYDEN, S. *De arte canendi.* Nuremburg, 1540.

HIRSCH, P. A. *Bibliographie der musiktheoretischen Drucke des Franchinus Gafori*, in J. Wolf-Festschrift. Berlin, 1929.

HOHN, W. *Der Kontrapunkt Palestrinas und seiner Zeitgenossen.* Ratisbon, 1918.

JACOBSTHAL, G. *Die Mensuralnotenschrift, des xii. und xiii. Jahrhunderts.* 1871.

JACOBSTHAL, G. *Die chromatische Alteration im liturgischen Gesange der abendländischen Kirche.* Berlin, 1897.

JEPPESEN, K. *The style of Palestrina and the dissonance,* 2nd Ed., corrected and enlarged. Copenhagen and London, 1946.

JEPPESEN, K. *Counterpoint, The Polyphonic Vocal Style of the Sixteenth Century.* London, 1950.

KIRCHERI, A. *Musurgia universalis,* 2 vols. Rome, 1650.

KOECHLIN, CH. *Traité de l'harmonie,* 3 vols. Paris, 1928–30. (In Vol. ii, Chap. 17, he discusses very fully the evolution of harmony from the ninth century to the present day.)

KRENEK, E. *Studies in Counterpoint.* New York, 1940.

KROYER, TH. *Die Anfänge der Chromatik im italienischen Madrigal des xvi. Jahrhunderts.* Leipzig, 1902.

KURTH, E. *Grundlagen des linearen Kontrapunkts.* Berlin, 1922.

LANFRANCO DA TERENTIO, G. M. *Scintille di musica.* Brescia, 1533.

LEICHTENTRITT, H. *Geschichte der Motette.* Leipzig, 1908.

LENAERTS, R. 'The 16th. century parody mass in the Netherlands', in *Musical Quarterly,* xxxvi, 1950, No. 3.

LIPPHARDT, W. *Die Geschichte des mehrstimmigen Proprium Missae.* Heidelberg, 1950.

LLORENTE, A. *El porqué de la música.* Alcalá de Henares, 1672.

LUDWIG, F. *Repertorium organorum . . . et motetorum vetustissimi stili,* Vol. 1. Halle, 1910.

LUDWIG, F. 'Die Quellen Motetten altesten stils', in *Archiv. f. MW,* 5, 1923.

LUDWIG, F. 'Die mehrstimmige messe des xiv. Jahrhunderts', in *Archiv. f. MW,* vii, 417–35, 1925.

LUNEBURGENSE, L. *Compendium musices.* Berne, 1546.

LUSITANO, V. *Introduttione facilissima et novissima.* Venice, 1561.

LUSSY, M. *Historie de la notation musicale* (in collaboration with F. David). Paris, 1882.

MACHABEY, A. *Histoire et évolution des formules musicales du 1er au 15e siècle.* Paris, 1928.

MACHABEY, A. *La notation musical,* Paris, 1952.

MAILLART, P. *Les tons ou discours sur les modes de musique.* Tournai, 1610.

MARTINEZ DE BIZCARGOLI, G. *Arte de cantollano contrapunto y canto de órgano.* Burgos, 1511. (Published again in 1528, and in Saragossa in 1531.)

MARTINI, G. *Esemplare ossia Saggio Fondamentale Pratico di Contrappunto sopra il canto fermo.* Bologna, 1774.

MARX, A. B. *Die Lehre von der musikalischen Komposition,* edition revised by H. Riemann. Leipzig, 1903.

MAY, HANS VON *Die Kompositionstechnik T. L. de Victorias.* Berne and Leipzig, 1943.

MENEHOU, M. DE *Nouvelle Instruction familière en laquelle sont contenus les difficultés de la Musique.* Paris, 1550, edited by H. Expert. Paris, 1900.

MENIL, F. DE *L'école contrapuntique flamande du xv. siècle,* 1815; revised and enlarged in 1906, under the title *L'école contrapuntique flamande au xvème et au xvième siècle.*

MERSENNE, F. MARIN *Harmonie universelle.* Paris, 1636.

MICHALITSCHKE, A. M. 'Studien zur Enstehung und Frühentwicklung der Mensuralnotation', in *Zeitschrift für MW,* 1929–30, xii, pp. 257–79.

MONTANOS, F. *Arte de música téorica y práctica.* Valladolid, 1592.

MORRIS, R. O. *Contrapuntal Technique in the Sixteenth Century.* Oxford, 1922.

MORTIMER, P. *Der Choralgesang zur Zeit der Reformation.* Berlin, 1821–23.

NASARRE, P. *Fragmentos músicos.* Madrid, 1700.

NASARRE, P. *Escuela música,* Saragossa. 1723–24.

NIEMANN, W. *Die abweichende Bedeutung der Ligaturen in der Zeit van Joh. de Garlandia* (Thesis. 1901, Leipzig).

ORTIZ, D. *Tratado de glosas.* Rome, 1553.

OTTOMARO, L. ARGENTINO *Musurgia seu praxis musicae.* Strasbourg, 1536.

PAREJA, R. DE *Música práctica* (1492), edited by J. Wolf. Leipzig, 1901.

PARRAN, A. *Traité de la Musique.* Paris, 1646.

PIETZSCH, G. *Studien zur Geschichte der Musiktheorie in Mittelalter,* i–ii.

PIONESAN, A. *La messa nella musica dalle origini al nostro tempo.* Turin, 1949.

PIRRO, A. *Histoire de la musique de la fin du xive siècle à la fin du xvie.* Paris, 1940.

PODIO, G. DE *Ars musicorum.* Valencia, 1495.

PONTIO PARMEGIANO, P. *Dialogo . . . ove si tratta della Theoria e Prattica di musica.* Parma, 1595.

PRAETORIUS, E. *Die Mensuraltheorie des Franchinus Gafurius.* Berlin, 1905.

PUERTO (PORTUS), D. DEL *Portus musical.* Salamanca, 1504.

RHAW, G. *Enchiridion utriusque musicae practicae.* Wittenberg, 1546. (H. Albrecht's facsimile edition, in *Bärenreiter-Verlag,* 1951.)

RIEMANN, H. *Studien zur Geschichte der Notenschrift*, Leipzig, 1878.

RIEMANN, H. *Die Mensuralnoten und Taktzeichen des 15. und 16. Jahrhunderts*, 2nd Ed. Berlin, 1906.

RIEMANN, H. *Kompendium der Notenschriftenkunde*. Ratisbon, 1910. (Sammlung, Kirchenmusik, iv–v).

RIEMANN, H. 'Verlorene Gesangene Selbstverständlichkeiten in der Musik des 14–15. Jahrh.', in *Rabischs Magazin*, 1907.

RIEMANN, H. *Geschichte der Musiktheorie*. Leipzig, 1921.

SANDBERGER, A. *Orlando di Lasso und die geistigen Strömungen seiner Zeit*. Munich, 1926.

SANSON, J. *Palestrina ou la poésie de l'exactitude*. Geneva, 1939.

SANTA MARÍA, T. *Arte de tañer fantasia*. Valladolid, 1565.

SCHMID-GÖRG, J. *Nicolas Gombert*. Bonn, 1938.

SERRANO Y AGUADO, G. *Explicación completa de la música polifónica de los siglos xvi. y xvii*. Madrid, 1904.

SOLER, A. *Llave de la modulación y antigüedades de la musica*. Madrid, 1762.

SPATARO, J. *Tractato di Musica*. Venice, 1531.

TAPIA, M. DE *Vergel de Música*. Burgo de Osma, 1570.

TIRABASSI, A. *La mesure dans la notation proportionelle et sa transcription moderne*. Brussels, 1924.

TIRABASSI, A. *Grammaire de la notation proportionelle et sa transcription moderne*. Brussels, 1928.

TORREFRANCA, F. *Il segreto del Quattrocento*. Milan, 1939.

TOVAR, F. *Libro de música práctica*. Barcelona, 1510.

URSPRUNG, O. 'Die Katholische Kirchenmusik,' in *Handbuch der Musikwissenschaft*, edited by E. von Bücken, Vol. ix. Potsdam, 1931.

VANNEO, S. O.S.A. *Recanetum de musica aurea*. Rome, 1533.

VINCENTINO, N. *L'antica musica alla moderna prattica*. Rome, 1555.

WAGNER, P. *Geschichte der Messe*, Vol. 1. Leipzig, 1913.

WINTERFELD, C. VON *Johannes Gabrieli und sein Zeitalter*, 2 vols. Berlin, 1834.

WOLF, J. *Musica Practica Bartolomei Rami de Pareia*. Leipzig, 1901.

WOLF, J. *Geschichte der Mensural-Notation von 1250–1460*, i–iii. Leipzig, 1904.

WOLF, J. *Handbuch der Notationskunde*, 2 vols. Leipzig, 1913–19.

WOOLDRIDGE, H. E. 'The polyphonic period', in *The Oxford History of Music*. Oxford, 1929.

YSSANDON. J. *Traité de musique practique*. Paris, 1582.

ZACCONI DA PESARO, L. O.S.A. *Prattica di musica*. Venice, 1596.

ZARLINO, G. *Soplimenti musicali*. Venice, 1588.

ZARLINO, G. *Institutioni et dimostrationi di musica*. Venice, 1602.

ZARLINO, G. *L'Istituzioni harmoniche*. Venice, 1573.

2. EDITIONS AND COLLECTIONS OF POLYPHONIC MUSIC

ANGLÉS, H. *La música en la Corte de las Reyes Catolicos*, I. Polifónia religiosa. CSIC, Madrid, 1941.

BÄUERLE, H. *Bibl. Altklassicher Kirchenmusik, in modernen notation*, 1903.

BÄUERLE, H. *La música en la Corte de Carlos V*. CSIC, Barcelona, 1944.

BÄUERLE, H. *El Cancionero Musical de Palacio*, Vol. I. Barcelona, 1947; Vol. II. Barcelona, 1951.

BORDES, Ch. *Anthologie des Maîtres religieux primitifs*. Paris, 1909.

CASIMIRI, R. *Anthologia polyphonia auctorum saeculi*, xvi. 2 vols. Rome, 1924.

CASIMIRI, R. *Repertorium Societatus Polyphonicae Romanae*, 6 vols. Rome: 1921–1934.

DAVISON, A. T. and APEL, W. *Historical Anthology of Music*, 2 vols. Cambridge, Mass., 1949–50.

EXPERT, H. *Maîtres Musiciens de la Renaissance Française*, 23 vols. Paris, 1894–1908. (An edition based on manuscript and printed music of the sixteenth century, with variant readings and historical and critical notes.)

FUENLLANA, M. *Orphenica lyra*. Seville, 1554.

GASTOUE, A. *Concert vocal historique, Piéces choisies de poliphonie religieux du ixe. au xve. siècle*. Paris, 1930.

HANDL (GALLUS), J. 'Opus musicum', by E. Bezecny and J. Mantuani, in *Denkmaler der Tonkunst in Oesterreich*.

LASSUS, O. DI *Opera Omnia*. Leipzig. (Begun in 1894 by Fr. X. Haberl and continued by Sandberger; 21 vols. have been published.)

MORALES, C. *Opera omnia*, transcribed and edited by H. Anglés; CSIC in Rome, 3 vols: 1, *Missarum liber primus*, 1952; 2, *Motetes*, 1953; 3, *Missarum liber secundus* (part 1), 1954.

MUDARRA, A. *Tres libros de música en cifra para vihuela*. Seville, 1546. Edited by E. Pujol. CSIC, Barcelona, 1949.

NARVÁEZ, L. *Los seys libros del delphin de música*. Valladolid, 1538. Edited by E. Pujol. Barcelona, 1944.

PAGELLA, J. *Anthologia vocalis*, 2 vols. Turin.

PALESTRINA, G. P. DA *Opera omnia*, Leipzig, 1862–1903. 33 vols. (Begun by Th. de Witt and continued by Fr. X. Haberl.)

PEDRELL, F. *Hispaniae Schola Musica Sacra*, 8 vols. Barcelona-Leipzig, 1894–8. 1, Morales; 2, Guerrero; 3, 4, 7 and 8, Cabezón; 5, Ginés Pérez; 6, *Fabordones* by various composers.

PISADOR, D. *Libro de música de vihuela*. Salamanca, 1552.

PROSKE, K. *Musica divina sive Thesaurus concentuum selectissimorum omni cultui divino totius anni juxta vitum ecclesiae catholicae*. Ratisbon, 1853–69.

QUEROL, M. *Cancionero Musical de la Casa de Medinaceli,* 2 vols. CSIC, Barcelona, 1949–50.

ROCHLITZ, F. *Collection de morceaux de chant,* 4 vols. Paris-Leipzig, 1835.

ROSTAGNO, J. H. and D'ALESSI, J. *Anthologia sexta vocalis liturgica,* 2 vols. Turin, 1928.

RUBIO, S. O.S.A. *Antología polifónia sacra,* Vol. I. Madrid, 1954.

RUBIO, S. O.S.A. *Canciones espirituales,* 2 vols. Madrid, 1955–6.

VASQUEZ, J. *Recopilación de sonetos y villancicos.* Seville, 1560. Edited by H. Anglés, Barcelona, 1946.

VICTORIA, T. L. DE *Opera Omnia,* edited by F. Pedrell, 8 vols. Leipzig, 1902–13.

I. Index of Technical Terms

II. Index of Music References

The use of bold type in this Index indicates that musical examples are to be found on those pages

III. Index of Names